In Search of
Jesús García

ISBN 0-9624499-0-3

Library of Congress Catalog Card Number 89-092257

This is the first publication of

Prickly Pear Press

Post Office Box 42, Payson, AZ 85547.

Proofed by Anne K. Dedera

Printed by Louis L. Lechuga of Budget Instant Printing

Design & Production by W. Randall & Deirdre A. Irvine

Randy's Art Works! / Great Characters!

DEDICATED to the people of Mexico

and Americans of Mexican descent

———

DEDICADO *al pueblo mexicano*

y a los estadounidenses descendientes de mexicanos

Jesús García

In Search of Jesús García

By Don Dedera

Prickly Pear Press

Post Office Box 42, Payson, Arizona 85547

Commemorative postage stamp, fiftieth anniversary, 1957

Contents

Foreword
Summer, 1976

My birthplace is Sonora. My adopted homeland is Arizona. Numerous members of my family live in Northern Mexico, while others are citizens of the Southwestern United States. Thus, most personally do I feel an international kinship.

Exactly how many persons of Mexican descent now live in the United States is difficult to estimate. According to the 1970 census, more than ten million Americans use (and sometimes mis-use) Spanish as their primary language. Through the mid-1970s it is believed that more than six million persons of Mexican parentage reside in the states of Texas, New Mexico, Colorado, Arizona and California. This is the largest concentration of people of Latin-American descent outside Latin America itself. In fact, after Mexico City, the biggest Mexican town may well be Los Angeles, California.

As so often happens when peoples and times change rapidly, some of the admirable elements of a culture are lost. By immigration or by birth, most of the people now known as Mexican-Americans are deprived important reminders of Mexico's greatness. Individuals from bilingual homes are generally educated in English language schools whose successful, handsome and heroic figures of history almost always bear non-Hispanic names. When a Mexican does appear in an American course of study, all too often the stereotype is of a surrendering Aztec, or of a raiding bandit, or of a bumbling general at the Alamo.

As a boy in Sonora I first heard of Jesús García. In later years as an instructor in Spanish at the University of Arizona, as a county attorney and juvenile court judge, as ambassador to Latin-American countries, I thought it a shame that García received so little acclaim north of the border. If noticed at all in a Sunday news feature, he might be called, "The Casey Jones of Mexico." Yet with all due respect, Casey just as correctly might be considered, "The Jesús García of the United States." I think it regrettable that for nearly seven decades after García's sacrifice at Nacozari there existed no celebration work in

I

English or Spanish of American publication.

So I applaud the appearance of this book. It tries to record in a factual manner the Nacozari episode and preserves a remarkable folio of scenes of frontier Sonora at the turn of the century. It is hoped that this book about the life and land of Jesús García will heighten awareness of the best of Mexico.

Raul Castro
Governor
State of Arizona

Note to the Foreword
Summer, 1989

Thirteen years have slipped by since Raul Castro so kindly supplied the foreword to *Goodbye, García, Adíos*. The points raised by the governor persist, if anything, more prominently than before. Hispanic populations continued to swell north of the border, and in the American Southwest people of Mexican descent now comprise the largest ethnic group of many communities. Bilingual education has become commonplace.

Governor Castro, now retired from public life, practices law in Phoenix, and enjoys a deserved reputation as a dinner speaker, for insightful advice enlivened by this sort of human anecdote: "Our first Arizona governor, George W.P. Hunt, served seven terms, and during his last term he came to my hometown, Douglas, for a political rally featuring free hot dogs. He was a huge man with drooping mustache, round eyeglasses, a white linen suit, and a pith helmet—a picture politician of his day. There I was barefoot and hungry. Governor Hunt gazed across the crowd and bellowed, 'Arizona is such a land of opportunity, why, some day one of these little Mexican boys may become governor.' It seemed as if he was looking straight at me. I remember saying to myself, 'I wonder when he's going to serve the hot dogs?' "

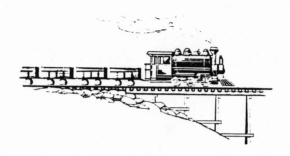

Preface

In early November, 1977, wire services flashed around the world a shocking newsstory under the dateline, Seoul, South Korea:

A freight train loaded with 30 tons of dynamite exploded in a ball of flame south of Seoul last night, killing 48 and injuring 1,280 persons, destroying 400 buildings and trapping another 700 persons under the roof of a fallen theater...

About 9,500 buildings—about 40 percent of all the buildings in Iri, a city of 120,000—were damaged. Preliminary police estimates put property losses at $10.7 million and indicated that 10,000 persons were directly affected, including many who lost their homes.

Initial fears that the losses would mount even higher were confirmed within a few days. Also the probable cause was revealed:

A security guard has admitted he fell asleep after drinking and left candles burning inside a dynamite-loaded freight car that exploded and killed 56 people and injured more than 1,300...

The blast Friday night leveled almost all buildings within a 1,000-yard radius of the rail station at Iri in central South Korea, digging a crater nearly 50 feet deep and leaving more than 10,000 homeless.

Police said Shin Moo Il, 36, admitted he left the parked freight car filled with 33 boxes of dynamite packed in wooden boxes to have a few drinks and on his return fell asleep without extinguishing the candles...

Officials said he told them he awoke to find his quilt on fire and the freight car filled with fire and smoke. He said he ran from the car, which exploded three or four minutes later.

Beyond the abstract sympathy felt for so many people killed, injured, and dispossessed in a far-away land, the tragedy piqued my interest in an unusual way. One year earlier had been published a book written by myself in English and translated into accompanying Spanish by a treasured amigo, Bob Robles. We named our bilingual book, *Goodbye, García, Adiós.*

García's dilemma remarkably coincided with circumstances prevailing in the Korean disaster. Almost to the day 70 years earlier, half a world away, this young Mexican worker likewise found himself in the center of a crowded community, at the railroad station, and aboard a blazing, dynamite-laden train.

Jesús García's train could have been the trigger to a blast even greater than Korea's. The Mexican train was loaded with four tons of American-made dynamite, but in an adjacent powder magazine were stored 500 tons more. Thus, the possible Mexican blast might have been 15 times stronger than the one seven decades later in Korea.

When researching my first book, I could only assume the peril that the powder house posed to the town. I did summarize the problem for a member of the San Diego, California fire department's bomb squad. Some of the factors he took into account:

- The community was densely populated.
- The townsite was a bowl-shaped valley.
- Near the train also were two enormous tanks of flammable gas.
- Chemicals, paint, and fuel were stored close by.
- The time of day, siesta, meant most residents were around town.

The crisis expert concluded, "I believe if the train had exploded... the magazine would have been struck by fire or shock. It would have become a gigantic bomb. What the flying boulders and concussion left standing, would have been consumed by fire. With the population concentrated at public places and work areas, casualties certainly would have numbered in the hundreds and probably in the thousands."

My first book about Jesús well might have been titled as this one, *In Search of Jesús García*. Not that the man was ever lost—certainly not in his homeland. His story clearly belonged to North America and the world. Yet outside Mexico's borders, with the passage of half a century, the facts and circumstances of García's sacrifice had become so distorted and commingled with legend, doubts arose as to whether the brave action had occurred at all.

In 1963 I was producing a daily column for *The Arizona Republic* in Phoenix when a reader sent a tear sheet from a railroad magazine. Without further research from the clipping I wrote my first brief version of García history. In a few days a valued friend telephoned: "It pains me to say this, but you have created the most inaccurate account I've ever seen printed about Jesús García. Your column contains a serious error in almost every line.

"What a shame! A man gives his life to save his entire town, and you are too lazy to get the story straight."

Coming from an ally, the criticism was doubly cutting. That very day I began a thirteen-year, off-and-on inquiry into the incident. As schedule and resources allowed, I traveled several times to Nacozari and to the capital of the state of Sonora, Hermosillo. While documenting details in those places, I learned that the story of Jesús García also had become somewhat garbled in his native land. For instance, an enduring, classic, popular railroad ballad misled Mexicans into believing that García died at the throttle of Engine 501, when indeed, he was the engineer of the much smaller narrow-gauge Engine No. 2. A minor matter perhaps, but illustrative of how adoring compatriots can be misinformed in song as well as prose, as a true event is revised by lyric and license.

Another surprise: I came to realize that the major amount of information about the life and times of Jesús García reposed in the United States. When American companies were sent packing in the decades after the Revolution of 1910, they took much of their business histories home with them. Railcars full of records, photographs and correspondence rolled northward from Nacozari, and eventually landed in American private scrapbooks and public archives. Notably rich in García-related material are the Douglas Collection and the University of Arizona, both in Tucson, and the Brophy family papers in Phoenix.

Because García was the employee of a major American corporation, inquiry bore factual fruit in Washington at the Library of Congress and National Archives. Other efforts in California and Arizona resulted in interviews of descendants of American company officials, and García's kin. A niece possessed a startling picture postcard of her uncle, seated on a camel, at the 1904 World's Fair in St. Louis. A 68-year-old nephew, in recalling that he was an infant in a crib in a house just a few yards from the Nacozari powder magazine, stated flatly, "If my Uncle Jesús had not done what he did, I would have died at age 10 days."

In all modesty my first book attained one goal: recognition of García. The book was reviewed favorably in dozens of publications. Big newspapers such as the *Houston Post, Sacramento Bee,* and *San Diego Union* splashed García in words and photographs in generous spreads. So, too, smaller papers: the *Brewery Gulch Gazette* of Bisbee, Arizona, the *Belvedere* (California) *Citizen,* and the *Boulder* (Colorado) *Camera.* García's deed gained attention in *La Confluencia,* the *Railway Journal, Sunset* magazine, and the *Hispanic American Historical Review.* Exxon Company U.S.A. purchased a thousand copies and placed them in every junior and senior high school in Texas with a substantial enrollment of Hispanic students. Phelps, Dodge Corporation presented a complimentary copy to one hundred-forty Arizona high schools.

Eventually revived awareness of García's heroism led to the first commemoration on the American side of the border in 1982 at the Pimería Alta Historical Museum at Nogales, Arizona. At the time Dr. Bernard L. Fontana, field historian of the University of Arizona, told the press: "It's only in recent years that a more general knowledge of García has developed on this side of the border." He attributed the latter-day renown to my book. From such a respected authority as Dr. Fontana, that was high praise indeed. Yet it is true that the book introduced García to Channel Four in Los Angeles, which aired a lovely tribute, and to Tucson's Davis Bilingual School, which adopted García as its "official favorite hero." This autumn of 1989 the Dons Club of Arizona plans to lead a travelcade of Americans to Nacozari to participate in the annual fiesta for García.

Doing such a figure justice proved an ever-humbling task for this writer. Despite my avowed dedication to accuracy, that first book about García contained its own errors, brought to light after publication. And fresh insights—such as those derived from the Korean disaster— now seem to justify an updated tribute to Jesús García, who unlike the hapless Mr. Shin, kept his wits about him and carefully calculated his options. Nor does this book presume to be the last word on the subject. The search for Jesús García should press on, because within his glorious moment shines that most precious of human allegory: the light of selfless love may redeem our darkest days.

For in the end, García more than saved his town. He reaffirmed the victory of the human spirit. No wonder that García is remembered in anecdotes such as this:

World War II was over. Its brave deeds were done. Three great men drew aside from a London dinner to talk about the past.

Their topic: favorite heroes.

Sir Winston S. Churchill was a historian of English peoples. He could choose among the valiant soldiers and sailors of a thousand years. Sir Winston himself knew valorous men in Cuba, India, Sudan, South Africa, and France.

Field Marshal Bernard L. Montgomery remembered courageous comrades at Dunkirk, Sicily, North Africa, Italy, and Normandy.

"Who is your favorite hero?" Montgomery asked Lewis W. Douglas, American ambassador to England.

Douglas, who had been cited for bravery in Belgium and the Argonne, could also draw upon a national roll of honor.

Yet without hesitation Douglas replied:

"My favorite hero is Jesús García."

Surprised, Montgomery said, "I have never heard of this, this... García!"

"Well, gentlemen," Ambassador Douglas responded, "let me tell you about him..."

Life in Old Nacozari. *Courtesy the Lewis W. Douglas Collection*

I. Old Nacozari

Ten years ago, when one stood in the center of Nacozari, and asked an elderly gentleman how many changes occurred during his lifetime, he responded:

"Oh, many. Considerable!

"See the new white houses on the tablelands. Over there the old mansion is half torn down. The railroad station is larger than when I was a boy. In the early days none of these noisy automobiles and trucks ran up and down Via Agua Caliente. Now Nacozari is smaller. Once there were 6,000 people here. Now there are 3,000. Nacozari has telephones and radios, and even electric refrigerators. North of the town is a small airfield, and occasionally an airplane lands there, with American tourists or Mexican officials. So many changes!"

But isn't it true that much remains the same?

"Oh, yes," the old man allowed. "Nacozari is still a frontier town. We are a thousand miles northwest of Mexico City. Nacozari lies near the border with the United States, one hundred thirty kilometers south of Douglas, Arizona. But the road is so bad sometimes it cannot be driven in less than five hours. Frequently the road is closed by floods, storms and fallen rocks. From Nacozari another road southward and westward is also long and crooked, across the mountains and plains to Hermosillo, the capital of Sonora."

A decade ago, as always, the homes and buildings covered a valley. Houses of wood, stone and adobe clung to the surrounding uplands. Customs endured. On washday the women of Nacozari adorned their fences with laundry to dry. *Cuando veas a tu vecino lavar, pon tu ropa a remojar.* "When you see your neighbor washing, put yours to soak." By tradition, the men of Nacozari did not work their small mines and farms and ranches on Sunday. They gathered to gossip on benches in the parks and along the sidewalks. At night the young people promenaded—boys in one direction and girls in the other—around the town square. Corn, the sacred food of ancient Mexico, was still honored by the children of Nacozari. Every autumn the first of the new crop of corn was popped, to resemble tiny white birds. Nacozari's youngsters scurried about to knock on the doors of friends with offers of snacks of warm popcorn.

"Little doves," they would shout. "Have some little doves."—*Palomitas, hay palomitas.*

Everywhere lurked the aroma of chili. The fragrance of the red pepper advertised a boardinghouse. There, one could dine upon flat, round cakes—*gorditas*, the little fat ones—stuffed with pork sausage and beans that were cooked on an antique wood burning stove.

Once more the elderly Nacozari guide was questioned, and he confessed:

"Of course, much remains the same. The rich copper mines are closed, but the concrete foundations of the industrial works are still rooted in the bedrock of Nacozari. There you can see the railroad where the trains plied between the town and the mountain mines. Sometimes, when I hear the donkeys braying from the oak trees at the edge of the town, I think Nacozari has not changed much at all.

"It is a peaceful, pleasant place, neither large nor small. Everyone is welcome. The people of Nacozari are proud. In all of Mexico no town celebrates a miracle such as that of Nacozari. On one day each year our entire nation looks to Nacozari."

"And why is this, old friend?"

"Once, the fate of Nacozari depended solely upon one of its citizens. In that desperate moment, Jesús García had to choose between life for himself, and life for Nacozari. What other town can boast of such a history and such a hero?"

In the decade since those lofty words were uttered, the aged hombre has died. If reincarnated, certainly he would be shocked at what has transpired in and around Nacozari. More change befell Nacozari in the 1980s than in the previous seventy years. Hundreds of millions of dollars were spent in developing *La Caridad*, "The Charity" low-grade, open-pit mine some twenty miles south of Nacozari. Although one of the largest copper mines in the world, La Caridad with its full production in 1988 could not fully supply the most modern of smelters near Nacozari. Boasting of a smokestack 942 feet tall, the smelter employed the latest in environmental safeguards,

In Search of Jesús García

including smokestack scrubbers and a sulphuric acid plant. Nacozari's position as a world leader in production of anode copper, copper concentrates and by-products seemed assured for decades to come.

As if overnight, automobile and truck traffic noisily rushed through and around Nacozari, as commerce and industry overwhelmed the town's more innocent days. Human waves of Mexican workers and South American refugees surged around Nacozari in their flight to the borderlands, in search of political asylum and work in Mexico's joint venture factories or Arizona's irrigated farms. Unlike much of Mexico gripped by poverty, Nacozari had jobs for many. Buoyed by high world copper prices, Nacozari boomed. The official population was placed at 18,000, but transients and casual residents possibly totaled that many more.

Yet for all the wrenching change, one constant remained.

Many years ago there lived a man named García of Nacozari.

To this day, in his honor, those names are reversed, to Nacozari of García, in Spanish, *Nacozari de García*. What caused this alteration of names?

For many centuries people inhabited the valleys of the river known as Moctezuma. Pieces of pottery and stone tools of prehistoric tribes littered the earth. Caves of the Oposura Range displayed age-old paintings upon their walls. The shady canyons and sweet springs around Nacozari made ideal village sites. The ancient peoples hunted deer, rabbit and quail, and harvested mesquite beans and acorns. Through the fertile valleys of Northern Mexico, many archeologists believe, thrived the arts of ceramics and propagation of crops, such as corn, squash and beans. The Sierra Madre Occidental provided the people with jasper and quartz, silver and gold.

Ancient legends tell of lost mines. But likely they were the same ones pounced upon by European explorers who pressed northward in seach of new territories for New Spain. Spanish documents three hundred years old tell of mining activities in the Nacozari area and surrounding highlands. Regarding the name Nacozari, it is believed to be scrambled Spanish for rich zone, *rica zona*. Or a perhaps a local word whose meaning is lost. On Father Kino's map of New Navarre of 1710, Nacozari appears as a mine camp. In neighboring Fronteras was born Juan Bautista de Anza, the daring captain who led an expedition from Sonora through Arizona to California and the Pacific Ocean in 1776.

The next century was a troubled time for the people of Sonora, and in fact for Mexico as a whole. Yaqui Indians and Spanish colonizers engaged in bitter combat. Independence from Spain cost more blood. Wars followed with the United States and France.

One of the ten major trails of the Apache and Comanche Indians passed by Nacozari. The plunderers would sweep across the international border, attack towns and ranches, seize what they could, and retreat to hiding places in Arizona and New Mexico. Alerted to danger by Nacozari's bugler, the men took up arms to defend their settlement. And afterward, too often the dead would be mourned in the Church of Our Lady of the Rosary. *Achaque quiere la muerte para llevarse a los mortales.* "Death yearns for an excuse to take mortals."

Even with the establishment of a stable central government, ninety-seven percent of the people remained poor. When General Porfirio Díaz became president in 1876, Mexico had little money of its own. The nation was deeply in debt. Acting more as a dictator than a president, Díaz invited wealthy foreign investors to establish new transportation and communication systems. Harbors were improved. By ship and rail the resources of Mexico—coffee, vanilla, lumber, rope, bananas, tobacco, sugar, minerals— were exported in exchange for the manufactured products of other nations.

Díaz held power for three decades. During that period the country emerged from debt. Those in high government office prospered. The government generated the money to promote economic advances. To the credit of Díaz, he suppressed crime and avoided war. The Strong Man of Mexico gave his homeland a generation of peace. Life was for the three percent of people who were rich and powerful.

In Search of Jesús García

The rest of the nation obeyed orders. Enforcing government decrees were loyal and sometimes ruthless units of city police and rural cavalrymen. Many were former bandits. Their method was "to catch in the act, kill on the spot."— *Cogerlos en el acto y matarlos al instante.*

Personal rights of jury trial, free speech and civil liberty were denied the people. A historian notes:

"President Díaz shut down every newspaper that dared to say anything against him or his government. His rural and city police broke up every meeting in which people tried to decide any important matter for themselves. Men who were popular and might become leaders of the people were thrown into jail or sent out of the country. President Díaz made his friends governors of the Mexican states. These governors put in their own friends as chiefs of the districts. The chiefs put in their own friends as mayors of the towns. So it came about in Mexico—which was supposed to be a democracy—that there was no chance for the people to choose the men who ruled them."

In these times, too, large land owners seized more and more farms and ranches. Many of these tracts were guaranteed by Spain forever for use by villagers. But laws were altered to make it possible for large land owners to grab up village properties. *Al que tiene potro le dan otro, y al que nada tiene le quitan.* "They give another pony to him who has one, and take another from him who has none."

Village workers were considered to be like children who required the fatherly discipline of owners. Some owners were cruel; others were kind. The workers earned so little (an average of twelve to twenty cents per day) that they were obliged to borrow from the owners. Some debts were passed down from father to son. If a worker ran away without settling his account, police pursued him and returned him in chains.

The workers of Mexico became slaves—to their debts.

The church in Moctezuma near
Old Nacozari

The 14-year old peon weighs 70 pounds
and carries 70 pounds

*Both photos, courtesy the
Arizona Historical Society*

7

In Search of Jesús García

A poor section of Nacozari around 1905 *Courtesy of the Arizona Historical Foundation*

United States President William Howard Taft and Mexico President Díaz
at a summit meeting in Mexico City *Author's Collection*

Rural police patrolled Sonora by twos and by troops
Upper right, courtesy of the Lewis W. Douglas Collection
Lower right, courtesy of the Arizona Historical Foundation

In Search of Jesús García

In Search of Jesús García

A bandit is executed not far from Nacozari
Courtesy of the Historical Collection of Herb and Dorothy McLaughlin

Small business prospered
as American industry
came to Nacozari
Clockwise, a bakery,
a cantina, a barbershop
*All photos courtesy of
the Lewis W. Douglas Collection*

Old Nacozari

Sailing ships stand at anchor
in the Sonoran harbor of Guaymas
Courtesy of the Brophy Collection

The line of cars was not long
at the port-of entry at Douglas,
nor was the line of people
at the customshouse
*Courtesy of the
Arizona Historical Foundation*

In Search of Jesús García

Old Nacozari

In just four years, 1899-1903, Nacozari grew greatly. Nearly all the industrial and building material was carried 90 miles overland by mule-drawn freight wagons from Naco, Arizona.

Both photos, courtesy the Lewis W. Douglas Collection

II. American Mexico

While a certain amount of liberty existed along the border, Nacozari, too, felt the influence of the Díaz government. The big difference was peace. Every family in the Nacozari area had been exposed to murder, kidnaping or robbery at the hands of American criminals, Mexican bandits and Apache raiders. The heroes of the people did not always win. Rather, they were persons who conquered fear, and rose above danger and pain. This typical Mexican attitude later was explained by the poet, Octavio Paz: "Much more than to victory we thrill to fortitude in the face of adversity."— *Nos estremecemos más ante la fortaleza de ánimo dando frente a la adversidad que a la victoria.*

For citizens of Sonora, as rurales began patrolling the highways, travel became safer; life and property, more secure. Now lawbreakers were punished. With government troops in Mexico and the United States cooperating, bands of Indian marauders were captured and pacified. When the Apache war chief, Geronimo, surrendered near the Mexican border to the American army in 1886, Nacozari welcomed the end of a dark and tragic night.

Toward the end of the nineteenth century, one word — copper — turned Nacozari from a tiny agrarian village into a bustling industrial center. At this time, particularly in Europe and North America, many mechanical marvels were invented and manufactured: engines, automobiles, farm machinery, power plants, electric motors, the telephone and the telegraph. Demand doubled and redoubled for copper vital to them all. The red metal also gained greater use in stills, cooking vessels, pipe, lightning rods, engraving plates, and, of course, as wire to conduct electricity. At the beginning of the 1800s the world's annual production of copper totaled less than 2,000 metric tons. In the next thirty years, production slowly increased to 4,000 metric tons. Fifty years later, world copper output amounted to 240,000 metric tons annually.

Not very far to the north of Nacozari copper mines were opened in Arizona, a territory which would become the forty-eighth of the

United States. Mines at Bisbee, Jerome, Morenci and Globe set a pattern for digging and processing the copper ore of this region. Thus, there came into being "a typical copper town." Work forces swelled with immigrant Slavs, Englishmen, Irishmen, Mexicans. In the better part of town were located hospitals, stores, libraries, schools and residential areas either financed directly by the copper companies or subsidized through taxation.

By modern standards working conditions were inferior. As the shafts sank to deeper and deeper working levels, the air turned foul. Walls of shafts and drifts could be dripping wet, or as hot as 150 degrees Fahrenheit. Some deep workings were so hot that a pioneer miner is quoted, "The sweat came out of the tops of your shoes." — *Se derramaba el sudor de los zapatos.*

The underground work was especially dangerous in mines operated by uncaring owners. Once, when an unscrupulous mine operator was criticized for scrimping on timbers to support the roofs of his tunnels, he replied cynically: "Men are cheaper than timbers."

A miner who lived through those times said of the work force: "There was lots of money and no one ever mistrusted anyone else. A man could walk into camp, a total stranger, and have a $20 gold piece for the asking of it, from the first man he met. There was no such thing as cheating in those days. It just wasn't done. The one who dared to do it was an outlaw... People's hearts were as large as a furnace door. They worked hard and they played hard, and they got the most out of life. I have seen some rather rough times here, but actually they were not bad. The men were rough in those days...but they were honest and they were strong."

Two North Americans were most responsible for recognizing the promise of Nacozari as a copper bonanza. One was Dr. Louis D. Ricketts, a tall, slender engineer usually dressed in threadbare khaki. He carefully surveyed the mineral claims of Northern Sonora, including the Pilares Mine, so named for rock formations resembling

In Search of Jesús García

pillars. The other expert was Dr. James Douglas, a Canadian experienced in geology and mining. On the advice of Drs. Ricketts and Douglas, Phelps, Dodge & Company bought the Moctezuma Copper Company in 1895. The next several years saw an expenditure of "a mint of money in a comparatively short time" by Phelps, Dodge to install hoists and build shops and warehouses. Also built were an ore concentrator, two furnaces and a gas plant. Mining activities were greatly expanded. The old camp — Nacozari Viejo — was abandoned in favor of a better location six miles to the north where a well-planned town was developed with permanent housing, sanitation, utilities and schools.

Incredibly, for most of a decade the materials for such construction were freighted as far as ninety miles in huge, high-wheeled, mule-drawn wagons. In turn, the reduced ore was shipped north in wagons eight feet tall. There would be three or four in tandem hitched together, with each wagon carrying five tons. By shouted commands and lashes of a blacksnake whip, a driver with extraordinary skill controlled a train of eighteen or twenty mules.

Such accomplishments were not much appreciated by the people of the big cities of America and Europe. But as historian Robert Glass Cleland noted, the transportation system for a great mine had to handle:

"The importation of thousands of tons of timber, fuel, explosives, machinery, hardware, tools, chemicals, and other supplies and equipment necessary for the operation of the mine and reduction works; the importation also of food, clothing, furniture, household articles, and all the kindred necessities with which the employees, their families, and the community about the mine must daily be supplied; and finally the export of huge quantities of ores, concentrates, matte, or kindred products to smelters, refineries and markets of the outside world."

Seeing Nacozari through its industrial expansion first was Dr. Ricketts, followed by James S. Douglas, son of Dr. Douglas. James, known as Jimmy to his friends, was self-taught in mining technology. As a youth he tried to cure an asthmatic condition by working on a farm in Manitoba, Canada. James S. Douglas managed the Moctezuma Copper Company from 1898 to 1910. Energetic, inventive, firm and fair, he gained a reputation as an efficient administrator and sympathetic patron of workers.

Eventually, Nacozari acquired not one railroad, but two. The first was hauled in by mule power. Engines, ore cars, rails, switches and construction material were divided into loads at the border town of Naco, and freighted across sandy washes, rolling hills and mountain passes to Nacozari. A narrow-gauge line was extended from the Nacozari concentrator to the Pilares Mine, six miles away.

Not until 1904 did the standard-gauge rails reach Nacozari. If ever a town adored its trains it was this one. There existed no distracting automobiles in those days. Not everyone could afford a horse and cart. The daily stage up and down the Moctezuma Valley was expensive, thus hitching a ride on a slow-moving freight became as natural to Nacozari as breathing. The highlight of the day was the arrival of the mainline train to Nacozari's new station. The moment became a social event.

Nacozari's adoration of trains is revealed in a story by Cuauhtémoc L. Terán.

"Their enthusiasm for the train has been such that once, on a Sixteenth of September, during the height of a patriotic speech by a well known and respected orator in the main plaza, at the sound of the train whistle the entire throng of patriots rushed to the railroad station, leaving their distinguished speaker speechless. It was at this point that the orator, halfway recovering from shock, muttered, 'Train lovers, sons of.... !' "

The Pilares Mine lay northeast, over bridges, curves, trestles, and tunnels. Sulphides of copper occurred within a volcanic formation a mile in diameter and 2,600 feet deep. At three to five percent copper content, the ore was not considered high grade in those days. Eight hundred miners wrenched the ore from the bowels of the earth. To forget their hard and risky work, off-duty miners retreated to a cluster of saloons at Pilares. Influenced by liquor, they frequently fought— and usually women were the reason.

Meanwhile, the sister community of Nacozari acquired a measure of gentility. Phelps, Dodge opened a large general store, and stocked it with quality merchandise. A social center containing recreational facilities, and a fine library were erected near the railroad station. The public buildings were open to every well behaved citizen. A billiard table graced one end of the library; a dance hall, opposite; and a one-room school, upstairs. High salaries attracted the best teachers to Nacozari's several schools for Mexican and American children. Men's clubs sponsored fiestas and dances for special occasions: New Year's Eve, the Fifth of May, the Sixteenth of September and Christmas Eve.

Justice of the Peace José B. Terán (nicknamed Don Pepe) provided Nacozari with local government. An appointee of the governor, Don Pepe served as mayor, police chief, and commander of the volunteer fire department. To this day in Nacozari the man is revered. He ruled with strength, wisdom, and mercy.

By 1907 Nacozari counted about 5,000 inhabitants. The new rails from the United States improved the values of surrounding, independent mines. Operators other than Phelps, Dodge were able now to sell their ores at a good price to American smelters. Farmers in the Moctezuma Valley began shipping some of their crops via the Nacozari Railroad northward to markets at Fronteras, and at the border ports of entry, Agua Prieta, Sonora and Douglas, Arizona. At the same time, the trains from the United States supplied the stores of Nacozari with factory-made clothing, packaged food and the best of tools.

The wealthiest of the fifty American families occupied homes on the north end of the west bank of the Nacozari River. Dormitories for bachelor workers filled flats of ground on the east bank. The Mexican community tended to concentrate to the south, although Nacozari by no means was a segregated community. Many Americans and Mexicans intermarried. In the river bottom Chinese families cultivated vegetables and fruits for the kitchens of Nacozari. In between rose numerous boardinghouses, some with public dining rooms, and all sorts of service and supply shops: pharmacies, barbershops, bakeries.

Some of the names of stores in a Mexican town might possess literary qualities:

A shop for secondhand goods, Don't Forget me in Passing. *No Me Olivides al Pasar.*

A butcher's, The Elegance. *La Elegancia.*

A pawn shop, The Mountain of Pity. *Monte de Piedad.*

A general store, The Fixed Price. *El Precio Fijo.*

A fruit stand, The Golden Husk. *La Cáscara de Oro.*

The names of saloons, The Dove, The Black Cat, The Little Rooster, I Am Laughing, Such is Life. *La Paloma, El Gato Negro, El Gallito, Me Estoy Riendo, Así es la Vida.*

In the latter places men might overindulge, and become intoxicated, or *ebrio*. And if *ebrio*, men might break the law a little or a lot. *Ebrio impertinente* was forgivable. *Ebrio indignado* was not. *Ebrio escandaloso* intimated a spectacle. *Ebrio rinas* involved a fight. *Ebrio lesiones*, a fight to victory. *Ebrio voltado*, passed out. *Ebrio orinando en la calle* translated into a relief of bladder in public. And deserving of greatest punishment, *ebrio insultos al gobierno*, drunk insulting the government. Such men earned a critical nickname: *barril sin fondo.* "Barrel without bottom."

Many an excitement grew from arguments about politics, horse races and romance. Fueling disputes was a beer, a fermented corn gruel called tesqüin, and other drinks derived from agave succulents: *bacanora, tequila, mescal, tenampa.* It is said that about the turn of the century three Nacozari residents were murdered by Yaqui Indians *ebrio*. A posse of townsmen gathered at La Paloma Saloon, set off ahorse, tracked down the culprits, and executed them by firing squad.

Otherwise, Nacozari took on airs of civilization with every passing year. Baseball teams of Mexican and American boys would go north by train to play teams at Fronteras, Cananea and Douglas. A track for horse racing was established on a reach of level ground. Women of the Green and Bohemian social clubs formed committees to assist the poor, to enlarge the library, to comfort the ill. Almost every Sunday there was a band concert in the town plaza.

Pay for the workers of Nacozari averaged about one American

dollar per day, equivalent then to about two pesos. That was five to ten times the national average. By comparison with other Mexican communities, Nacozari became so prosperous that it acquired its own pet name, *de El Real*, because business there could be on a cash basis, in silver coins.

An American might says of old Nacozari—money talks. As Mexicans might say— *Con dinero hasta la mona baila.* "With money, even the monkey dances."

Naco baseball team played with a stick and string ball
Courtesy of the Lewis W. Douglas Collection

Nacozari shipped its copper to Douglas, Arizona for smelting
Courtesy of Arizona Historical Foundation

At nearby Bisbee, American miners carried candles and
lunch buckets into the Copper Queen Mine
Courtesy of Arizona Historical Society

Dr. Louis D. Ricketts

Dr. James Douglas

Twenty-four
mule teams such
as these freighted
nearly all of American
Nacozari southward
from Arizona
*All photos,
courtesy, Arizona
Historical Society*

In Search of Jesús García

Americans had a free rein in turn-of-the century Sonora. Clockwise from left, an American hunter and his Mexican helper bring home fat turkeys
Courtesy of the Historical Collection of Herb and Dorothy McLaughlin

Americans brand cattle on their Mexican ranches.
Courtesy of the Brophy Collection

Dudes from New York enjoy an outdoor Mexican holiday
Courtesy of the Historical Collection of Herb and Dorothy McLaughlin

James S. Douglas shows skill with a shotgun *Arizona Historical Foundation*

31

Library, Nacozari Sonora, Mexico.

Pride of Nacozari was its stone library
Courtesy of the Arizona Historical Foundation

Six mules pulled the Moctezuma Stage to the Nacozari Hotel
Courtesy of the Lewis W. Douglas Collection

The brick headquarters of the Moctezuma Copper Company was still standing in 1989
Courtesy of the Lewis W. Douglas Collection

1. Site of Commisario's House

2. Jail

3. Rooming House

4. Site of Catholic Church

Courtesy of the Phelps Dodge Collection

Jesús García at his favorite pastime, horseback riding. *Courtesy of the Douglas Collection*

III. Jesús García the Man

From all over Mexico's northern states—Sonora, Chihuahua, Durango, Coahuila, Sinaloa—industrious citizens were attracted to *El Real*. For them Nacozari represented a way to break free from the drudgery of debt.

They had heard that the mining company paid above average and promoted productive workers. Through these years no more than fifty positions were filled by Americans in the mines, shops, warehouses, concentrators and railroads. The majority of the machinists, carpenters, mining bosses, timber setters, storekeepers, teamsters, plumbers and mill hands were of Mexican nationality.

At this hub of activity in 1898 arrived a widow, Mrs. Rosa Corona viuda de García and her eight children. Her daughters were Trinidad, Angela, Artemisa, and Rosa. Her sons were Francisco, Miguel, Manuel and Jesús, the youngest, born November 13, 1883. Their father, Francisco García-Pino, died on the journey to Nacozari, probably of a burst appendix. He had been a blacksmith in Hermosillo, and at Batuc, another mining town. Young Jesús, as an apprentice at his father's forge, learned the basics of metallurgy and mechanics. Since early childhood he displayed an ability with machinery.

The biographers of Jesús García mention these other boyhood traits: courteous, studious, quick-witted, friendly, popular. It is written that as a schoolboy Jesús one day listened intently to his instructor lecturing on Mexican history and patriotism. Jesús blurted, "Some day, I, too, would like to be a hero and do something for my country."

Certainly he was generous. From his father he earned an allowance, which he usually spent on his friends. He lived the Mexican adage, *A lo dado no se le da fin.* "A gift has no end."

A name of affection given to Jesús was *El Güerito*— The White One—a term Mexicans sometimes attach to a person of fair complexion.

Despite the death of Mr. García, the mother brought her children to Nacozari in hopes there would be work for herself and her mechanically talented sons. They all quickly found work.

The family was not poor. They had the money to build a house in the Incline Neighborhood, so named for the 700-foot-long tramway at the Pilares Mine. Some of the García boys gained work in the mines. The Incline Neighborhood was noted for its carefree lifestyles, numerous fiestas, and occasional violent disagreements.

An excellent cook, Mrs. García was persuaded to open a small restaurant. In this cafe Jesús began as a fulltime working man. He fetched the mesquite and oak wood for the iron stove, hauled out the ashes, swept the rough board floors, whitewashed the sun-dried, adobe brick walls, washed dishes and waited tables.

Everyday fare included tortillas of wheat flour, and beans simmered with chunks of beef or pork. Light breakfasts — *los desayunos ligeros*— were of sweet rolls, or cinnamon-flavored pastries, usually with coffee. Perhaps a more substantial breakfast would be eggs, country style. In the afternoon Mrs. García would cook *posole*, hominy-with-meat. Her other specialties were sweet pastries, and vegetable and meat soups. Like many women of Sonora doña Rosa enjoyed preparing snacks called *antojitos*, literally meaning, "little whims." On feast days she might prepare roasted beef or venison, or wild turkey, or tamales and enchiladas, stacked like pancakes as preferred in Northern Sonora. Never was the García kitchen free from the fragrance of oregano, cumin, chili, coriander, onion, cheese and cinnamon.

Yet struggle though she might, Mrs. García did not profit greatly with her cafe. Jesús, as he approached manhood, found part-time employment. He swept out stores, hauled off refuse, and ran errands in the Incline Neighborhood. It was the unhappiest period of his life, but he never lost his hope.

"You are a little bit less than a man," his brothers kidded him, — *Todavía no llegas a hombre.*

"Patience. Every dog has his day," Jesús would retort, — *A cada perro se le llega su día.*

When he was seventeen Jesús took matters into his own hands. He put on his best clothes and went directly to the office of the railroad boss, W.L. York. York had a reputation of toughness.

"I can do better with my life," he told Mr. York. "The work I am doing now is beneath me."

York was amused, but at the same time, impressed by the youth's wish to improve his lot. Said York, "Don't take on something you can't finish, Whitey."

And Jesús insisted, "If only you would permit me to wipe the locomotives, I could be a more valuable person."

As reporter Frank Aley wrote years later in the *Douglas Daily International*, "Admiring the boy's sense of honor, York gave him employment as a water boy. Ever alive and devoted to his duty, García gathered promotions. He was next given a shovel, then placed with the section gang (to maintain a section of railroad track). He was made a brakeman, and from that he rose to fireman, and from that (at age twenty) became locomotive engineer.

With promotions came raises in pay. In time Jesús helped move his mother and family to a better house with running water and electric lights, in Nacozari. A corner house, it had a large screened porch in front, and a garden with fig trees out back. By coincidence, a near neighbor was Jesús García's schoolmaster from Batuc, Manuel Armendariz, now a magistrate in a Nacozari court.

So satisfied was the railroad company with the work of Jesús that in the spring of 1904 he was awarded an all-expense-paid trip to the World's Fair in St. Louis, Missouri. His companions were Rafael Rocco and Cibriano Montaño, mechanics; Jose Vejar from the concentrator; Zacarías Ruíz and Heraclio Ramos of the supply warehouse department; Ignacio D. Montaño, electrician; and Francisco Ancira and Manuel Vázquez from the company store. A store official, S.H. Casey, led the excursion. During this vacation in St. Louis Jesús climbed into the cab of one of the largest and newest railroad locomotives, and he handled it with ease.

As romanticists, Mexican men of that day were unrivaled. This characteristic permeated Jesús to his soul. He wore a cowboy hat, tilted back. He was an expert horseman. Sometimes he grew a mustache; impulsively he would shave himself clean. Often he dressed up in white shirt, coat and tie. He did not hide his intentions, which were to impress the maidens of Nacozari.

Toward this goal he frequently hired the most famous musician of Nacozari, Silvestre Rodríquez. This man was not only a musician of first rank, but a composer as well. He wrote *Your Glance, Sighs and Tears, Green Eyes*, and a ballad that won international appreciation, *The Man from the Coast*. Paid by Jesús, the orchestra of Mr. Rodríquez would venture into the night to sing endearing sentiments beneath the windows of the most beautiful young women of the town. In perfect harmony the musicians played the trombone, violin, bass fiddle and flute.

One of the loveliest lasses of Nacozari was María de Jesús Soqui. By the autumn of 1907, when Jesús García was nearly twenty-four years of age, he and Jesusita were engaged. On the evening of November 6, despite the early signs of a cold, wet storm approaching, Jesús once again summoned the music men. The orchestra and singers filled the entire town with melody. Especially for Jesusita they sang, until she responded with hot chocolate and the sweet bread, *pan dulce*.

"How can we ever afford to be married?" she teased Jesús. "You're spending all your money on serenades!"

"But I have an incomparable love affair," he answered — *Pero yo tengo un amor incomparable.*

And later, strolling home, his last words to Mr. Rodríquez were:

"Put this on my bill, my friend. I promise to pay you in full very soon."

Very soon Jesús García would pay all his debts, a thousand times over. For of this repayment, *Entre dicho y hecho, hay gran trecho.* "Easier said than done."

8

One of several of Nacozari's musical bands pose for a portrait
Courtesy of the Lewis W. Douglas Collection

Jesús García the Man   41

Jesús García's father was a blacksmith, much like this Sonora craftsman
at the turn of the century
Courtesy of the Historical Collection of Herb and Dorothy McLaughlin

Inset, Jesús García's mother, and sister, Rosa
Courtesy of the Collection of Mrs. Norbert L. Sammelman

Above, the Incline Neighborhood at the Pilares Mine where the García
family made their first home
Left, El Porvenir and the bottom of The Incline
Both photos courtesy of the Lewis W. Douglas Collection

Above, when the García family prospered, they moved to a better neighborhood in Nacozari *Courtesy of the Lewis W. Douglas Collection*

Inset, Jesús and his sister, Angela *Author's Collection*

In Search of Jesús García

Above, packing supplies horseback from Arizona to Nacozari
Courtesy of the Brophy Collection

Left, the 1904 St. Louis World's Fair the best workers of Nacozari share an
all-expense-paid holiday. Jesus Garcia is seated on a camel third from left
Courtesy of the Collection of Mrs. Norbert L. Sammelman

11. Stone Warehouse   13. Concentrator Well
12. Train Station

Nacozari in 1907 when the Library was being erected. Some men already are at work repairing railroad tracks
Courtesy of the Phelps Dodge Collection

IV. Jesús García the Engineer

An early twentieth century frontier Mexican mining town tended to waken one life, one lumen, one moment at a time. At false dawn skinny Nacozari dogs bawled at coyotes yipping at the outskirts of the community. Sleek ravens on scimitar wings squawked insults as they contested for scraps from Nacozari kitchens. Roosters saluted a morn's glow delayed by iron-gray overcast.

A few lights had glowed all night. Crews at the powerhouses remained awake to peer at their meters and operate the machinery to reduce wood and coal into flammable gas. Stored in gigantic tanks, the gas was burned to make steam, to drive turbines, to generate electricity for the copper mill and town lights.

The telegraph at the railroad station was connected both to Douglas, Arizona and Hermosillo, Sonora, but the instrument sat silent for hours. Under the glare of a single lamp the ticking station wall clock lulled the station agent to sleep. It had been a quiet night for the police department and for Gabriel Fimbres, chief of the rural lawmen. All was serene at the Nacozari hospital. This Thursday, November 7, 1907 was another day for Nacozari to rise and ready for work, which for most began at seven o'clock. *Si quieres vivir sano, acuéstate y levantate temprano.* "If you aspire to be healthy, early to bed and early to rise."

The day was charged with omens. Smoke from domestic chimneys hung like a shroud across the valley. Exhaust vapors from the tall industrial stacks darkened the heavy, sodden air. Church bells calling to the faithful pounded Nacozari with leaden, hollow groans. An abrupt chill signaled the end of Indian Summer. Soon would arrive the season of soaking winter storms.

Bachelor workers in coats and capes departed their dormitories, ate light breakfasts of beans and corncakes, then scattered to their places of work. Even for bustling Nacozari, this day began with an uncharacteristic measure of anxiety. The town was uncomfortably crowded with extra laborers building a new concentrator downriver of Nacozari. The copper company's general manager was absent on business, and mine superintendent J.S. Williams bore doubled responsibilities. He hurried his breakfast of ham and eggs and appeared early at the red brick headquarters of the Moctezuma Copper Company.

Martín Corrál also had cause to hustle. Soon Mr. Williams would be inquiring whether the carpenters were busy. And Mr. Corrál was chief of carpentry. It was much the same for Antonio Elizondo and William Chisholm in the machine shop. The erection of the new mill was quickening the search for more ore reserves, and stacks of samples in the assay office awaited analysis by Miguel Quiroz and Rafael Moreno. Tomorrow would be payday, and Susano Montaño was expected to have the Mercantile stocked full. The town called *El Real* soon would be spending its cash.

Although Mexican in language and spirit, Nacozari submitted to a North American concept of time. "The schedule" was all-important. "Hard work never hurt anyone," said the bosses from the North. Everything was affected by the schedule. The hospitals, the schools, the library—all adjusted to the strict work shifts. Even peddlers of firewood and powdered chili and garden produce were obliged to adjust their lives to the schedule. *Una mano lavala otra y las dos lavan la cara.* "One hand washes the other, and both wash the face. All for one and one for all."

Jesús García, too, made haste. This day he was expected to take his train several times to Pilares. Without sleep Jesús went home to change into his working attire: boots, denims, and cowboy hat. He paused in his mother's kitchen for a bowl of tripe soup— *menudo*— recommended for clearing the cobwebs of alcohol from the brain.

Mrs. García also spent a sleepless night. A woman of sixty years of good and bad luck, she was deeply superstitious. She dabbed at her eye with a corner of her apron.

"I worry about you, my son," said she.

"But, Mom," Jesús answered. "The music was delightful, and the girls were so beautiful, we forgot how late it was."

"It is not your partying that concerns me. All through the night the dogs of Nacozari were howling, and the roosters were crowing...a sign that someone in our town will die today. Your own dog, Spotty, howled the most. You must be very tired. Something tells me that you should not go to work today."

"I must go, Mother. Just the other day Mr. Douglas was telling me how much he depends on me. He said if I keep up the good work, I have a chance to become the chief engineer of the mine railroad."

"Then be careful, my boy. Go with God."

At six o'clock Jesus García approached the roundhouse of the narrow-guage railroad near the center of Nacozari. Antonio M. Elizondo was yawning in the doorway.

"Did you sleep well last night?" asked Jesús.

"Not one wink, Whitey," answered the master mechanic. "A band of madmen were bellowing all night in the streets of Nacozari."

"Those beautiful songs. You did not enjoy the music?"

"What is sublime music to one, may be intolerable noise to another. You know that even though they are both made of clay, there's a difference between a potty and a pot." — *Pues ya lo sabes, que aunque son del mismo barro, no es lo mismo bacín que jarro.*

"I should charge you money for the concert," laughed Jesús. But he had little time for jesting. The locomotives of the mine railroad were not large, but they were just as difficult to operate as the big ones.

There were three engines, all manufactured by Porter of Pittsburgh, Pennsylvania. The largest weighed about thirty tons. In railroad jargon two of the locomotives were designated 0-6-0, meaning that there were no smaller wheels either in front or behind the six large driver wheels. Thus, for maximum pulling power, all the weight was borne by the drivers. Adding to the tonnage was water stored in a tank which wrapped like a saddle around the boiler. Either wood or coal was the fuel, carried on a steel rack affixed to the rear of the cab. A smaller 0-4-0 locomotive was usually kept at Pilares, for switching cars and making up trains.

Jesús' locomotive was Number Two, Built to order in May, 1901, it was more handsome now than the day it was delivered. On his own time Jesús had added painted ornamentations, and polished the copper and brass. For holidays and fiestas Jesús would decorate his engine with tricolor flags. In the spotless interior was a special place for a photograph of Jesusita.

Many small but important chores went with running such a locomotive. On top of the boiler was bolted a dome which Jesús and his crew kept filled with dry sand. From that dome sand could be dropped onto the rails to provide traction.

An hour previously a watchman had started a new fire under the boiler. Then the regular fireman, José Romero, took over. Gradually he increased steam pressure. He greased rods, pistons, axels and other mechanical parts. He topped off lanterns and torches with signal oil. While José fetched drinking water, Jesús took inventory of the tool chest: hammer, wrenches, chisels, hooks, flares.

The locomotive was ready to leave when two brakemen, Agustín Barcelo and Hipólito Soto, reported for duty.

"We will not have a conductor today," said Agustín. "Albert can't work."

"What's wrong with Old Man Biel?"

"He's sick, in the hospital."

The news was not good. Albert Biel was a German, a railroader of long experience. A conductor served as overall boss of a train and its crew. He received and carried out orders from superiors. He oversaw switching and loading operations. He was the one who said when a train might move, and when it must stop. On this day the absence of the conductor meant more work for everyone.

Jesús made the best of it, saying, "Well, that puts me in charge of the train again, correct?"

"For sure." — *Desde luego.* And José added, "Sing and don't worry, my friend." — *Canta y no llores, mi amigo.*

Jesús manipulated levers and valves. Brakes released, with a steamy cough the engine chugged away from the roundhouse. The train backed downriver, reversed direction, and headed uphill to Puertecitos, a half mile from the center of Nacozari and six hundred feet higher in elevation. Jesús had changed the tune of the train whistle with wooden plugs, and as his engine disappeared through the pass, he warbled a farewell message:

"Till we meet again, young lady!"

In a few minutes the locomotive huffed into the upper train yard known as *El Seis*, Number Six. Here were storage sheds, and houses for families of men who maintained the railroad tracks. When not in use most of the rolling stock of the mine railroad was parked on sidings at Number Six. Now Jesús coupled onto a string of twenty empty ore cars. By tradition, anyone could ride free on the train. Miners returned from leave. Women visited relatives. Children went sightseeing in the open cars. With a clang of bell and screech of whistle, the train began the snaking, chuffing journey six miles to Pilares.

The mine perched two thousand feet higher than Nacozari. The track curved and climbed through great granite mountains. Timber trestles as tall as one hundred twenty feet bridged deep ravines. In other stretches the rails bent sharply on a roadbed blasted from bulging slopes. Elsewhere the Pilares line darted through hardwood canyons teeming with birds: robins, scrub jays, roadrunners, masked bobwhites, turkeys. In such habitats Jesús saw deer, wolf and mountain lion. As well as black bear he caught glimpses of rare grizzly, and once, the fleeting movement of a spotted jaguar, the largest cat of the New World.

Such experiences were fewer for José Romero, the fireman. He worked bent over, to heave fuel into the firebox. Jesús metered out the power with throttle and other controls. With whistle and hands he signalled instructions to the brakemen.

To make it possible to burn wood fuel safely, the locomotive was fitted with a "big head" smokestack in which sparks were killed with baffles and screens. But on this day, on the steeper grades, Jesus noticed that a few live cinders were escaping the stack. He yelled to José:

"Remind me tonight to tell the mechanical department to repair our stack, okay?"

At 7:45 the train reached Pilares. Invariably, mock insults were exchanged between the crew of the railroad and the workmen at the ore bins.

"What happened, Whitey? You are late. Surely, you weren't keeping Nacozari awake last night?"

"Well, I hate to tell you," Jesús answered. "But I was. Our original plan was to go serenade my Jesusita. But we passed by a certain balcony, and a gorgeous young woman asked us to sing for her. We remained there a long, long time."

"Who was she?"

"Your sweetheart!" shouted Jesús.

"Ah, Whitey, you know how to hurt a man." – *Ay, Güerito, cómo te gusta herir el corazón.*

The ore emerged from the tunnels in small, hand-pushed cars, and was dumped into wooden bins. When chutes were opened below, the ore tumbled into the open gondola cars. Then the little engine at Pilares took the cars down to a switching area called El Porvenir, where with link-and-pin couplers trains were prepared for descent to Nacozari. Jesús needed only to drop off his empty cars, couple onto twenty full cars, and head down the mountain.

Given the heavy loads and steep, tortuous grades, the return trip was more demanding. A clumsy engineer could break his train in two. No fun, to try to outrace or play tag with a string of runaway cars! Brakemen also required sharp skills. If they set a brake too tightly, wheels would lock, slide, and wear a flat spot.

Railroading in 1907 was filled with surprises, of wet rails, of loose crossties, of animals on the tracks. Especially pesky were the wild donkeys. A standing order to all engineersof the Nacozari Railroad was to maintain speed and collide with the donkeys, if need be. It was the one command which Jesús García did not have the heart to obey. Whenever possible, he stopped his train, and heaved sticks of wood or lumps of coal at the donkeys to make them move.

Other perils loomed. Once a train of the Pilares mine rounded a particularly tight curve. A length of rail had been pried from the ties. The engineer and his crew jumped to the ground. None was injured, but the locomotive careened off the track and overturned, crushing the cab roof and other extremities. Repairs required weeks in the Nacozari machine shops. The culprits, suspected of seeking revenge for some reason, were never caught.

Again, in October, 1906, Jesús was running a train that lost its brakes not far from Nacozari. He commanded his crew to leap free, and they spilled off the accelerating cars. If Jesús had jumped, the train might have sped into the heart of Nacozari without warning, most likely to plunge—engine and car after car, into the concentrator. Jesús remained with his locomotive. He reversed the wheels and dropped sand onto the tracks. He thundered down upon the yard at Number Six, grit shooting under the back-spinning wheels, sparks showering from the rails, screeches wailing from the whistle. García's grim contest with gravity came to a standstill, exactly four meters from the end of the line.

But today, the descent was routine. Jesús eased the train into Number Six. From a switchback he shoved the ore cars around a hill and onto a trestle overhanging the ore crushers. The cars were designed to tilt on swivels to unload the cargo. In short order the brakemen emptied the ore into tall, concrete bins. Then it was time again to go to Pilares.

Cuando andes en la silla, maneja bien. "When you are in the saddle, ride it." Or, keep a good thing going.

On steep grades en route
to the mine at Pilares,
Engine Number Two
emitted enormous
clouds of smoke

Jesús García was in line to
be promoted to chief
engineer of the narrow
gauge railroad

Train photos,
courtesy of the
Lewis W. Douglas
Collection
Jesús García
author's collection

The ore at Pilares Mine was rich enough to pay for expensive underground tunneling. Extracting the ore deep within the Earth was difficult and sometimes dangerous work. *Both photos, courtesy of the Lewis W. Douglas Collection*

Miners and residents of Nacozari were free to ride the train between Pilares
and Nacozari, and one of the thrills was crossing a timber trestle across a gorge
more than a hundred feet deep *Courtesy of the Lewis W. Douglas Collection*

Once the train was wrecked by saboteurs who were never caught *Courtesy of the
Lewis W. Douglas Collection*

15. Concentrator

16. Ore Bins and High-Line

17. Train for Pilares

18. Smelter Stack

19. Smelter

20. Compressor House

21. Gas Generator

22. Briquette Plant

Had not García succeeded
in stopping the runaway train,
it would have plunged off
the elevated track marked
16-17 into the concentrator
and smelter works below
Courtesy of the
Phelps Dodge Collection

This is the train of Jesus Garcia plying an elevated track above
the old ore concentrator
Courtesy of the Lewis W. Douglas Collection

V. The Desperate Deed

Time: one o'clock. Jesús García was pleased with the course of the day. Following his second round trip, his locomotive again rested at Number Six. With luck, he might complete two more runs. A messenger swung aboard and relayed an unexpected order.

"They need supplies at the mine. Take the train to the lower level and talk with Mr. Elizondo. You will need five cars and he knows what the freight will be."

Jesús left fifteen of his gondolas at Number Six, and descended to the lower yard. As explained by Mr. Elizondo, boxes of dynamite

totaling four tons would be transferred from the powder magazine to two of the ore cars. During the loading operation the train crew would break for lunch.

To shatter the rock, the mine at Pilares consumed great amounts of explosives. The most powerful type of dynamite was obtained at Oakland, California and shipped by rail to Nacozari. The explosives were stored in a stone-and-mortar building close to both of Nacozari's railroads: the standard gauge to the United States, and the narrow gauge to the Pilares mine. On this day the magazine contained two thousand boxes of dynamite. Also nearby was warehoused the explosive caps and fuses to detonate the dynamite. Gingerly, a crew of laborers began to fill the cars with explosives.

"Be careful with those boxes, boys," Jesús advised the warehousemen. "Handle them as if they were angels from heaven."

"Or we will all be angels in heaven, eh, Whitey?"

"In heaven?" joked Jesús. "I'm not certain that all my friends will go to heaven!"

— ¿En el cielo? No creo que todos mis amigos vayan al cielo.

As Jesús strode homeward, he could perceive every element of Nacozari. The town had no trolley, no automobiles. So most everything necessarily was within walking distance. He passed the busy offices of the mining company, workshops, storehouses. The afternoon nap, siesta, was a luxury that Nacozari mostly abandoned in order to keep "the schedule."

The Nacozari River roared with runoff from the mountains. Jesús, while walking across the bridge of the mainline railroad, glanced downstream to the new concentrator rising like a Mayan temple on the left bank of the river. On the other side huddled commercial establishments, cafes, shops. Jesús greeted Father Francisco Navarrete. The segregated schools for American children and Mexican children were in session. Some of the Peraza brothers were in town. They operated the mule-drawn freight wagons until the railroad pushed down from Arizona, and they became standard gauge railroaders. Now Leonardo Peraza greeted Jesús:

"Hey, Junior, where's your little toy train?

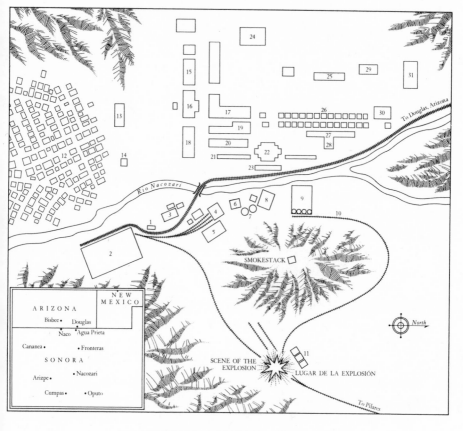

NACOZARI, SONORA, MEXICO

Circa 1907 — Simplified, not to exact scale

1. Dynamite	. . . . . *Dinamita*		15. Apartments	. . . *Apartamientos*
2. New concentrator	. *Concentradora nueva*		16. Boarding house	. . *Casa de huéspedes*
3. Carpenter shop	. . . *Taller carpintería*		17. Hotel	. . . . *Hotel*
4. Round house	. . . . *Casa redonda*		18. Warehouses	. . . . . *Bodegas*
5. Warehouse	. . . . . . *Almacén*		19–20. Schools	. . . . . *Escuelas*
6. Gas works	. . . . *Generador de gas*		21. Old apartments	. *Apartamientos viejos*
7. Gas tanks	. . . . . . *Gasómetro*		22. Library	. . . . . *Biblioteca*
8. Smelter	. . . . . . *Fundición*		23. Railroad station	. *Estación de ferrocarril*
9. Old concentrator	. . *Concentradora vieja*		24. Stables	. . . . . . *Establos*
10. Railroad to concentrator	. *Ferrocarril a la concentradora*		25. Douglas house	. *Casa de familia Douglas*
11. El Seis	. . . . . . *El Seis*		26. Residences	. . . . *Residencias*
12. Residences, commerce	. . *Residencias, comercio*		27. Warehouse	. . . . . *Almacén*
13. House of Don Pepe	. *Casa de Don Pepe*		28. Store	. . . . . . *Tienda*
14. Jail	. . . . *Cárcel*		29. Manager's house	. *Casa del administrador*
			30. Hospital	. . . . . *Hospital*
			31. Power plant	. . . *Casa de fuerza*

The jest drew laughter from Jesús Lugo, watching from the door of his library. Billy King, secretary to Ben Williams, smiled. Also enjoying the exchange were Carlos C. Soto and Francisco Gallego, who were picking supplies in Nacozari for the Lampos Mine.

Jesús was almost home when he was stopped by John Chisholm, a boy of mixed bloodlines, nicknamed *El Mestizo*. The boy informed Jesús that he was playing hookey from school and wished to ride the train to Pilares. Jesús couldn't say no. He told the lad to catch the train at Number Six where the empty cars were spotted.

At home Jesús found his mother more distressed than before. She had prepared his favorite meal—chicken soup—not the bland broth known north of the border. This *caldo de pollo* was mounded with joints of meat and whole vegetables; carrots, potatoes, onions, But not from peeling onions were Mrs. García's eyes moist with tears.

"I thought I would never see you again alive," Mrs. García told Jesús. "Never have I had such a strong premonition. Now the roosters are crowing in the middle of the day."

Jesús strove to quiet her fears, saying: "But Mother, everything is going perfectly well at work. Two more trips to the mine and my day will be done."

"It looks like it's going to rain," said Mrs. García.

"I'll have a roof over my head, Mother. And if I do get wet, I won't melt."

"Still, you should take your mother's advice. I've told all my women friends of my worries. They also believe you should not go back to work."

Later, many of Mrs. García's friends would recall her blue mood. But Jesús could not heed her warning. The train crew already was one man short. With soft words and a robust hug, he consoled his mother. Then he set out for the train yard. Over his shoulder he threw a reassuring farewell:

"Until later, little mother, goodbye."— *Hasta mas tarde, mamacita, adiós.*

"Take care, my son." — *Cuidate, m'hijo.*

In Search of Jesús García

Two o'clock. In the lower yard, the loading of the freight was completed. In inspecting his locomotive Jesús was mildly annoyed in discovering that the yard workers had allowed the fire to dwindle, resulting in a loss of reserve steam pressure. It took time to rebuild the fire. Perhaps this was enough to distract the engineer's attention from another, more serious, error. It was the rule of the Nacozari Railroad always to put cars with explosives at the rear ends of trains. On this train, the laborers loaded the dynamite on the first two cars, next to the engine. The arrangement would not be allowed by a conductor, but on this day there was no conductor.

Impatiently, Jesús helped José Romero stoke the fire. Slowly steam pressure built. Then, expending as little power as possible, Jesús backed the train out of the yard onto a switchback. The muggy wind from the north toyed with swirls of smoke and steam. A brakeman threw a switch, and Jesús opened the throttle for the uphill run, most of it a steep, four percent grade. As the locomotive labored, it sent up smoke and ash. Now the wind was reinforced by the gathering speed of the train. Live sparks from the faulty smokestack flew across the engine and cab to land on the first two cars, among the dynamite boxes.

At first the fire was not noticed by the train crew, rather by passers-by. A small Mexican boy shouted an alarm, but his tiny voice was lost in the chuffs of steam. It was an anonymous American man who was heard, in rude Spanish:

— ¡Oye, mira ahí, humo en el polvo!

"Hey! Look! There! Smoke in the powder!"

Francísco Rendon was a train brakeman, not on duty. Now on his day off he was hitching a ride to Pilares.

"Try to douse the fire!" bellowed Jesús.

"Slow the train!" responded the brakeman.

Francísco had an idea. On this stretch of track there was no water. Fanned by the breezes of the train's motion, the smoldering increased. If Jesús would stop the train, Francísco would pull out the smoking dynamite box, lower it to the ground, and smother it with earth. Francísco hooked an arm under the box. As the train slowed, he lifted the box a little. For the moment the plan seemed to be working. Then fresh air flowed between boxes—some said from bales of hay—and open flames burst upward, driving Francísco away from the car. Francísco and the other brakemen removed their jackets and attempted to beat out the flames. The fire spread. Intensified.

During the desperate struggle not far away Jesús García's sweetheart was embroidering pillow cases for her hope chest. A ten-day-old nephew, Herb Sanchez, dozed in a crib in the home of Artemisa Bartlett only a few yards from the powder magazine. Mrs. Ben Williams, at her home on the opposite side of the valley, was nursing the seedlings of a winter vegetable garden. James, a four-year-old son of the general manager was playing on the floor of Nacozari's largest house. Their lives, all the lives of Nacozari, abruptly were at risk.

When hope vanished for squelching the fire, Jesús opened the throttle and called for his crew to jump off and save themselves.

He was remembered as saying, "Get away. Leave me alone!"

And, "I'm going to run my luck."

And, "Tell Father to say Mass for whatever is left of me."

And, "I go to my death." — *Me voy a mi muerte.*

José, the fireman, pleaded. "Let me take the train. You have a family. I have no one."

"No. I am the engineer," insisted Jesús. "Save yourself."

At the García home the mother detected the note of urgency in the wild whistling of the train. She went to a window and watched the engine increase speed up the grade and around the curve. Under her breath she said to herself:

"Son, you are traveling too fast...."

Obeying the orders of Jesús, José Romero jumped off the train. He rolled off the roadbed into the brush. Miraculously he landed near a culvert where he hid.

A hundred meters farther, the train came into view of Number Six. The upper yard had no warning. Fifteen-year-old John Chisholm was standing by the side of the track. Four Mexican miners lounged against empty ore cars, awaiting a lift to Pilares.

Jesús and his locomotive climbed through a shallow cut. Train and engineer needed to go but another fifty meters to a flat grade where Jesús might turn the bomb loose and leap for his life. Opposite this shallow cut, just twenty meters away, rambled sheds and other frame buildings housing eight families of section hands. María and Trinidad Gutierrez heard the unusual wailing of the whistle. They went to their window. Frantically, Jesús waved his cowboy hat and shouted words they could not understand.

The sisters raised their hands to return what they assumed were friendly gestures. Through the glass they smiled at Jesús García, their enthusiastic friend. And although they would live many years more, this vision would be their last.

Time, two-twenty.

So enormous was the explosion, the dynamite cars vanished entirely.

Jesús was killed in an instant, hurled against the front of his cab. Much of the engine was blown away, and the body of Jesús fell between the rear wheels.

A jolt like an earthquake shook Nacozari. Despite the protection of the hill, a shock wave shattered window panes all over town. Dishes shook off tables and out of cabinets. The four-year-old Douglas boy would never forget the boom. It was heard ten miles from Nacozari. Mrs. Williams rose from her gardening to sway with the rumble of echoes, and to follow the flight of metallic debris and rocks from the center of a boiling cloud of smoke and dust. Mrs. Williams watched a rain of shrapnel pound upon Nacozari, piercing roofs, stampeding livestock, driving citizens to cover. As if in a trance, Mrs. Williams tracked an object across the sky to land at her feet. It was a tortured sculpture of two rails, twisted and fused together. Onto a mountainside two and a half miles east of Number Six was hurled a portion of an ore car.

Panic gripped the people of Nacozari.

"The gas tanks blew up!"

"It was the powder magazine!"

"No. The dust and smoke are rising from Number Six."

Together with some of his mounted deputies, Don Gabriel headed for the upper yard on horseback. On foot, Don Pepe organized a rescue posse. En route to Number Six they met a man crying, "Go back. The gas tanks are ready to let go!" The rescue detail retreated in disorder. Then, regaining courage, the men again rushed up the train tracks, only to encounter Hipólito Soto, brakeman, babbling as if insane:

"The powder! The powder! It exploded! Everything is gone!"

So shocked was Hipólito, his friends were obliged to lead him like a child to the hospital. — *Le falta un real para el peso.* "He lacks the change to make the dollar," the friends tell the nurses. "He's crazy in the head." Up the hill still farther the posse met José Romero, deafened and dazed. Without a pause he also repeats himself, "He ordered me to jump. I wanted to stay, but he ordered me to jump."

Thomas C. Romney was near the center of Nacozari, bossing construction of tenements for an influx of workers for the new concentrator.

Later he wrote an eyewitness account:

"I observed a train of cars winding its way...the train seemed to be on fire. I watched it with interest and with considerable curiosity until the last car had passed over the summit of the hill when almost immediately there occurred the most terrific explosion that I had ever witnessed. The force of the concussion was so violent that it seemed to me my head would be blown from my shoulders and as if by instinct I found my hands locked over the top of my head to keep it from being blown into space.

"After the shock was over, I went at top speed to the summit of the hill to discover what happened.

"The sight...haunts me still...a dead man lying on his back with the warm blood from his body flowing down the hill in a small rivulet...the warehouse...so completely demolished that not one particle of evidence remained...even the solid shelf of rock on which the building stood received a scar fully three feet deep. Off to the left... had stood a tenement house that had sheltered several families. Not one stick of timber was in its original position."

In Search of Jesús García

The carnage at Number Six was such that Don Pepe fainted at the sight of it. The four lounging miners were killed. The Chisholm boy, struck dead by a bullet-like rivet, lay two hundred meters from the spot where he stood waiting. The wrecked lumber of the section houses covered the bodies of seven women and children. Eighteen other residents and workmen of the upper yard were injured.

The people of Nacozari swarmed to the rescue. Most helpful were off-duty miners, trained in first aid. They applied tourniquets, splinted fractures and bandaged wounds. Wagons carried the injured to the hospital.

In awed silence, survivors marveled at the wreckage of the train. The engine was dismantled. Cars obliterated. Cab destroyed. The engine was off its tracks, teetering on the rim of a crater. Jesús was identified by his boots. It was the duty of the brothers and brothers-in-law to recover the body and take it home...home to the mother who was so certain that tragedy would touch Nacozari that day.

By late afternoon the darkening sky crackled with lightning. Nacozari flinched as thunder echoed among the ageless mountains. A cloudburst more ferocious than anyone could remember washed clean the gore from Number Six, and lashed the greater town saved from catastrophe by Jesús García.

In the hospital, the doctors toiled through the night with the injured. An American nurse hovered over José Romero, the shell-shocked fireman. The ringing in his ears began to diminish. He heard the tempest, and whispered:

"Even the heavens cry tonight."— *Esta noche hasta el cielo llora.*

Nacozari at about the time of its crisis, showing the bowl-shaped setting of the town. The main line and narrow gauge railroads converge in the right, foreground, and near the juncture is the stone powder house containing 2,000 boxes of dynamite. García took his burning train up the hill and out of the picture to the right
Courtesy of the Lewis W. Douglas Collection

In Search of Jesús García

Miners pose for a group portrait at the Pilares Mine. In the cab of the donkey engine is García, enlarged, inset *Courtesy of the Lewis W. Douglas Collection*

The Desperate Deed

The large picture was taken from the end of the track elevated above the old concentrator. Enormous gas tanks can be seen at the left. The danger of the tanks to the town was dramatically demonstrated when once, a tank caught fire, and consumed itself
Courtesy of the Lewis W. Douglas Collection

5. Hotel Nacozari
6. School House (Now García Monument)
7. Casa Grande (Now Staff House)

8. Manager's Residence
9. Foundations of Library Building
10. Site of General Office

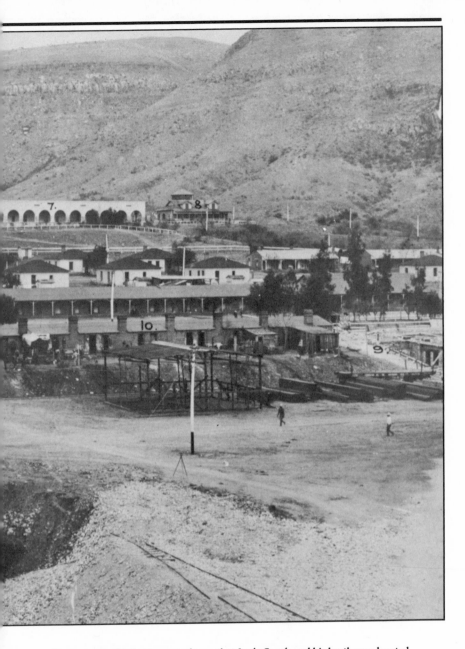

It was near to this better part of town that Jesús García and his brothers relocated their widowed mother from the poor Incline Neighborhood
Courtesy of the Phelps Dodge Collection

Doubtful, that any of these Mexican and American schoolchildren would have
survived, had García's train exploded in the center of Nacozari
Both photos, courtesy of the Lewis W. Douglas Collection

"El Seis" 220 P.
Explosion 4 tons dynamite

13

Nov. 7 1907

Killed

The handwriting is that of Lewis S. Douglas, and the scene, that of *El Seis* just twenty minutes after the explosion. the wrecked locomotive huddles in a cut to the left, and the section houses lie flattened, center. Nacozari was just across the hill behind the smokestack   *Courtesy of the Lewis W. Douglas Collection*

Nacozari's splendid monument to Jesús García was dedicated November 7, 1909 at ceremonies including the serenading of the hero's brother (in suits) and sisters (in white dresses), at left of large photograph
Large photo, courtesy of Mrs. Norbert L. Sammelman
Small photo, courtesy of the Special Collections, University of Arizona Library

VI. Goodbye, García, Adiós

Seldom are heroes created in the very moment of their valor. Battlefield reports of a soldier's courage may belatedly reach his nation. Years may be required to prove the value of a wonder drug, and bring honor to its discoverer. From political leaders and literary figures, history may withhold glory for generations.

Even in reverent and sentimental Mexico, homage has not been paid immediately. In his time Cuauhtémoc was not honored nationally. Relatively few contemporaries realized the importance of the freedom fighting priests Miguel Hidalgo y Costilla, and José María

Morelos y Pavón. Benito Juáres, Zapotec Indian who led the war of reform, was not widely understood. Only gradually was national fame accorded the six Child Heroes, who in 1847 defended Mexico City against the invading Americans. The Revolution's gallants evolved: Madero, Carranza, Obregón, Zapata, Flores-Magón. Francísco (Pancho) Villa was dead forty-three years before the Mexican Congress declared him a hero.

But not one day passed before Jesús García was proclaimed a hero. James S. Douglas, general manager of the Moctezuma Copper Company, was at Cananea, another Sonora mining property, when at 4:00 p.m. November 7, he learned of the accident. By special train he traveled day and night via Douglas, Arizona, to arrive at Nacozari at 1:25 a.m., November 8. He found the town wide awake and eager to fill him in. As soon as he understood what had happened, he telegraphed:

> *Governor Luis E. Torres*
> *Hermosillo, Sonora*
>
> *Esteemed General:*
> *Seventy boxes of dynamite caught on fire by flying sparks from the locomotive yesterday at 2 p.m. at the time the train was leaving the lower yard of Nacozari via the narrow gauge railway. All the employees jumped from the train except the locomotive engineer who remained aboard to prevent the train from rolling back and exploding in the lower yard.*
> *Explosion occurred at the moment the train entered the upper yard, in front of the section house. Eight women and children living in the section house, as well as five men, including the engineer, perished. They were all Mexican nationals except an American boy. Engineer was a native of Hermosillo and had worked on the same locomotive seven years. He died heroically....*

Later the same morning Douglas posted a letter to General Torres giving further details:
There were 2,000 boxes of dynamite stored in the warehouse,

and if the explosion had occurred there, the number of victims would have been frightening....When the fireman yelled for him to jump, García answered by saying that if he did, the train might roll back toward the concentrator, and remained aboard the locomotive, intending, evidently, to reach the upper yard and run on through toward the mine in order to clear the section houses. His action was most heroic, for if indeed he had abandoned the train, it would have rolled back, and if the explosion had occurred at the bottom of the hill, the damages to the machine shop, stored powder, offices as well as the concentrator, would have been dreadful. The fireman and brakemen also exhibited great courage in attempting to pull out the box of powder, which was smoking among the rest of the càrgo, and in holding out until it started to burn....

Following a thorough report of the circumstances, including a casualty list, Douglas concluded:

This terrible misfortune is a source of grief, but the courage exhibited by the entire crew helps one bear the burden to a certain extent. The young Jesús García, in particular, can be considered a hero.

The story made newspapers throughout the world. Although initial dispatches contained errors that would be repeated for years, they immediately recognized García's exceptional sacrifice. On November 8 the *Douglas Daily International-American* devoted most of its front page to:

HEROISM OF MEXICAN SAVES NACOZARI
**Deliberately Gave Up Life In Performance of Duty
Perished, With Fourteen Others,
While Taking Burning Train of Dynamite Out of Camp.**
Long after the attendant horrors of yesterday's terrible explosion at Nacozari, when fourteen or fifteen lives were whiffed

out, have been forgotten, and the bodies of the victims have crumbled into dust, the heroism of a Mexican engineer, Jesús García, who took the burning train, heavily laden with dynamite, out of the center of Nacozari, knowing that it would explode at any moment yet standing by his post in order to save the concentrator and other property in the city until death came to him, will be remembered—or should be. His matchless bravery and devotion to the highest conception of duty stands out in bold relief in the tragic occurrence of yesterday and will compare with any exploit in the annals of history....

Less ponderous was the dispatch which appeared on Page One of the Tucson, *Arizona Star* on November 9:

ENGINEER'S BRAVERY SAVES MANY LIVES
He Tried to Get His Train Out of Town
To Prevent Explosion There
(Special to *The Star*)

NACOZARI, Nov. 8—That the concentrator and a good part of the town of Nacozari are not now in ruins is due to the bravery and heroism displayed by Jesús García, who was the engineer on the ill-fated train that was wrecked here yesterday afternoon by the explosion of two cars of powder that were part of the train.

The train consisted of four cars, the two nearest the engine being open and loaded with powder. Two cars immediately behind these two were heavily loaded with baled hay. It was feared by the trainmen that owing to the size of the load some of the hay would topple off the cars. Consequently two bales were placed on the cars loaded with powder. A spark from the engine fell upon the hay and it was soon ablaze.

The fireman, whose name could not be learned, looked back and noticed the blazing hay...cried to the engineer and begged him to jump from the train. The cars, however, were at that time just passing through the town of Nacozari, and the engineer realized that if the explosion occurred near the town, a good part

*of the place would be destroyed and hundreds of lives lost.
Realizing this, the brave man called to his fireman to jump, which
the latter did, and the engineer then put on a full head of steam
and started away from Nacozari. Owing to his quiet wit and
wonderful display of nerve, the train was at least a half mile from
the town when the frightful explosion occurred.*

*The train at the time the powder exploded was passing
through a small Mexican settlement and several houses which
were located beside the track were blown to the ground, killing
ten of the occupants....*

Through the night of November 7-8 a wake was held for Jesús.
A line of visitors—as if all the community, filed past the casket in the
García home. The rich and poor, lowly and mighty, young and old paid
their respects. Maestro Rodríquez excused himself early to go home
and write a composition, *Jesús García,* for his orchestra to play at the
funeral. James S. Douglas appeared among the mourners. Jesús
had been a frequent guest at the Douglas home, he being a
companion of Douglas' son, Lewis. Together the young men rode
horses and played baseball. At the Douglas home, Jesús García was
considered more like a son than just a friend.

In his book, in Spanish, *Jesús García, the Hero of Nacozari*,
author L. Teran Cuauhtémoc states that James S. Douglas stood for
a long time at the casket of his favorite employee, and "his fixed eyes
seemed to look beyond the body as though reviewing the many
occasions he had enjoyed this man's company. And as his tears rolled
one after another down his cheeks, he managed to praise his friend,
'Jesús, you are indeed a hero.' " —*Jesús, eres un verdadero héroe.*

There is an American saying, "No matter how important a man,
the size of his funeral usually is determined by the weather." Despite
drizzles threatening more downpour, the crowd at Nacozari's old
cemetery on November 8 possibly numbered in the thousands.
Professor Monzón attacked President Díaz in his funeral speech.

"The time has come for the working men of Nacozari," he began
in a vibrant voice. "We gather here to render last homage to a worker

who has become a hero by setting an example of fearlessness and self-denial; our country needs men of such mettle, and examples of the courage to recover our civic rights which day by day we see trampled by a reproachful and despotic dictator."

For a full year Nacozari went into mourning, solemnized by black dress and cancellation of dances. The name of the town was changed officially from Nacozari to Nacozari de García. In time, streets, bridges, schools, parks, section houses and union halls were named for García throughout Sonora, Mexico and Latin America. There came into being ballads, poems, and essays lionizing Jesús. Social clubs were named for him in Mexico City and in Los Angeles, California. Sadly, the multiplying tributes could not comfort the sweetheart of Jesús. For all of his jesting (once he told her, "I don't know which I love the most—you or my locomotive.") she loved the man passionately.

Within the year of community mourning and personal, unrelieved melancholy, Jesusita, too, expired. Her doctor blamed "heart trouble," which Nacozari construed to mean "a broken heart."

Jesús was revered in other countries as well as his own. The American Cross of Honor, founded in May, 1906, by an act of the U.S. Congress, was awarded with the citation:

Whereas, Jesús García sacrificed his life in order to save those of the inhabitants of Nacozari, Sonora, Mexico, the Board of Governors of the American Cross of Honor has passed the following resolution— That history reveals very few instances of acts of such great valor, or of such heroic deaths; and no honor bestowed can be too large to commemorate the memory of this hero who died for his fellow men. It is hereby agreed that this resolution be recorded in the minutes of our meeting, and that a copy be sent to his Excellency, the Mexican Ambassador in Washington.

In Search of Jesús García

Eventually, monuments were raised for Jesús at Hermosillo, Mexico City, Zacatecas, Veracruz, Tapachula, Guadalajara, Mazatlán, Naco, Aguacalientes, Cuidad Obregón, Empalme, San Luis Potosí, and Tierra Blanca. Near the junction of Benjamin Hill, Sonora, where the *Pacífico de México* meets the rails from Mexicali, there is a narrow gauge locomotive enshrined to the memory of Jesús García. Other monuments to the man were dedicated as far away as Cuba, Guatemala, England and Germany.

Fittingly, the most handsome of monuments was reserved for Nacozari itself. With $5,000 contributed by the Mexican government and substantial donations by private citizens and the copper company, a memorial was erected remindful of that for Admiral Nelson in London. It is a single column, some thirty feet tall, of gray granite, on a square base. On one side of the base is a bronze plaque bearing a likeness of Jesús, beneath the coat of arms of the Republic of Mexico.

When the monument was unveiled on November 7, 1909, dignitaries were present from Sonora, Chichuahua, Arizona and other states of Mexico and the United States. Nacozari schoolgirls bore flags of every nation; boys in uniforms sang and marched; a troop of cavalry formed an honor guard. The town was decorated as never before. The American patriarch of Nacozari, Dr. James Douglas, delivered the eulogy. The speaker also tried to explain how the accident happened. Perhaps his company had been criticized for the way in which the train was loaded. Was hay with the dynamite, or not? Should dynamite cars be covered? Did fuses and caps accompany the explosives? There was even a hint of, *Cuando el gato no esta, los ratones están de fiesta*, "When the cat's away, the mice will play." Dr. Douglas seemed to be aware of rumors and accusations:

The love of life is the strongest implanted in our nature. It is the impulse which conserves the very existence of the race, and therefore, when the individual is willing to part with his life for the life of others, he is performing an act of self-sacrifice, impelled by the highest motives. On the other hand, when men become so cowardly and selfish that they will not voluntarily endure suffering or face death in defense of their rights, or better still, for the protection of their fellow men, they are unworthy of citizenship in a free country. It is true that every soldier who joins the colors recognizes that he may at any moment be called upon to run the risks of being killed in battle; but it is a remote risk. And when the critical moment arrives, his courage is fortified by the presence of his comrades and by the terrible excitement of the struggle.

But there was no such stimulus to nerve Jesús García to perform the heroic act which this monument commemorates. He was the engineer of a train of cars bound from the lower yard at Nacozari to the mines at Pilares. On the grade overhanging the power house and the works and in full view of the town, he saw that a car of dynamite was on fire. Instead of putting on the brakes and jumping, he turned on full steam and calmly gave instructions to the brakeman to extinguish the fire. They, like the brave men they were, stood by their post until García himself bade them leave the train and leave him to his fate. On he rushed with the blazing cars and the load of infernal powder. The speed of the train fanned the flames, but he hoped that the volcano behind him would not explode until he had reached the spot where a bluff between the train and the town would shield it and its people from inevitable destruction. He had barely reached the goal when the explosion occurred. The town was saved.

Its savior would have reprobated the honor we are bestowing on him. He was doing his duty, and what else could he do? Such were Jesús García's feelings as he stood with his hand on the lever and his eyes looking steadfastly into eternity.

But we need the encouragement of noble examples and to be reminded of our own duty. That is why we gather around this monument commemorative of a noble deed and a hero's death.

At the time the tragedy occurred, the old concentrator was in commission. The railroad is a three percent grade going up from the concentrator and a car released before it reaches the divide and passes over would inevitably roll back into the reduction works.

On the seventh day of November, 1907, it devolved on García in the usual course of his duty to pull the ore train from the Nacozari concentrator to the mine.

It appears that the American conductor was indisposed and was off duty that day, and that particular capacity was not represented.

One hundred and sixty boxes of giant powder were to be transferred that day from the magazine at Nacozari to the mine, on this train. It was the usual practice, of course, to swing the powder cars to the rear.

This day there were six cars of merchandise, and the powder filled two cars. These cars were open and unprotected as ore cars always are.

In switching, García made a mistake, for which he subsequently heroically atoned with his life. Instead of switching the powder cars to the rear, they were coupled up next to the engine. That was a fatal mistake, but he had not had training in the capacity of a conductor; he was simply an engineer, and young at that.

As he started up the first leg of the Y the wind was such that it blew the sparks away from the train, but when he stretched out on the next leg, the wind was facing him and blew the sparks away from the train, but when he stretched out the next leg, the wind was facing him and blew the sparks back on the cars. Being a three and one-half grade, the engine labors heavily and your contributor can testify to the severity of the cinder storm which falls on the first two cars.

The current story that a bale of hay was on one of the cars is pure fiction.

Another hero of the incident who escaped and who deserves the greatest measure of credit, is Francísco Rendon, who, after the fire started, attempted to pull the burning box of powder away, but was unable to do so for the reason that it was jammed... Rendon was a brakeman, but on this occasion he was not

like the former Mexican province of Alta California, was sometimes blessed with two governors at a time and once with triplets," Carranzistas, Villistas, and the followers of various other revolutionary jefes, Yaqui Indians, and plain bandits rode up and down the unhappy state and to and fro in it, looting, destroying, and extracting tribute as they rode.

"All in all, however, in spite of a few temporary shutdowns, many inconveniences, and a prolonged period of uncertainty and strain, the Phelps, Dodge properties below the border suffered relatively little from the years of banditry."

Train service north to Douglas occasionally was interrupted. Villa attacked Agua Prieta in April, 1915, and many people in Nacozari, including five hundred company employees and some relatives of García, fled across the line to Douglas and Bisbee.

Nacozari was hard hit by the influenza epidemic of 1918. The early 1920s brought a postwar depression in copper prices. At least a thousand families, more than 4,500 people, drifted away by wagons and trains in 1931 following the world economic collapse. In *Copper's Children*, Inez George Horton, described the scene:

Besides all the worn-out, broken-down furniture these people could gather together...they bought stove wood a day or two before their departure and insisted in throwing it in, too.

Pieces of lumber, corrugated iron roofs, windows and doors were removed from company houses to be hauled away at company expense.

Full-size bed-springs danced up and down on a little burro's back to the accompaniment of kitchen pans beating time against the sides of a wash-tub on another little burro trotting behind.

Trunks, sewing machines, chairs, tables, bureaus, iron beds, and iron stoves waved perilously in the air and we have not heard yet how the four little legs under them kept balance....

The mines of Nacozari revived to supply World War II, which

cleaned out Pilares to a depth of 2,600 feet. Then, another economic slump, this one lasting decades. But in the past ten years Nacozari has staged another comeback. Today, twenty miles to the south of Nacozari, yawns La Caridad, one of the world's ten largest open pit copper mines. Other mineral deposits in the area have been exploited. A gigantic, modern smelter extracts the red metal from great volumes of concentrated ore. By some estimates 30,000 people now reside in and around Nacozari.

García's day of glory has been reconsecrated every year in Nacozari. His mother attended the annual ceremonies until her death in 1924, at age seventy-seven. By custom, brothers and sisters, cousins and second cousins have traveled from their homes in Hermosillo or Los Angeles or Agua Prieta or Yuma, Arizona, for the services. The relatives are treated as guests of honor in Nacozari de García.

Until recent years, also, it was traditional for a special train carrying as many as eight hundred people to depart Agua Prieta for Nacozari. Of a typical recent year during the three-and-a-half-hour trip, refreshments were served and *mariachis* played and sang, *Heaven Dropped You on Me*, and *What a Big Heart You Have*, and *The Eye of Glass. Me Caíste Del Cielo y Mucho Corazón y El Ojo de Vidrio.* Following a banquet Jesús García Day climaxed with the presentation of the Mexican colors in front of the Nacozari Hotel. Columns of boys and girls in blazers marched to the music of a drum and bugle corps.

A chorus sang Mr. Rodríguez's composition lasting five minutes—one minute of march, one of hymn, one of dance, one of ballad, and the final minute of march: "Oh, grand benefactor, your name is immortal and will live forever in our hearts." — *O, gran bienhechor, tu nombre es inmortal y vivirá para siempre en nuestros corazones.*

Thirty wreaths were placed, each occasioning a speech. Alfredo Kaldman, an elderly engineer, fired up the engine on the square, calling for yet another rendition of Engine 501. Then the hundreds of celebrants climbed back on the train to Agua Prieta and Douglas for another round of beers and more from the *troubadores:*

Remembrance of Ipacarai, and *The Lost Child. Recuerdos de Ipacarai y El Niño Perdido.*

But aside from all the pomp and ceremony, aside from all the flowery speeches, aside from all the exquisite monuments, Mexicans have contrived for the hero of Nacozari the ultimate in tributes. And it is this: In Northern Sonora, in the huddled communities best acquainted with the desperate deed, when someone must bid farewell to a lover, or to an aged mother, or to a most-cherished brother, or to a revered godparent, he or she may say:

"Goodbye, Jesús. Goodbye, García." —

Adiós, Jesús. Adiós, García.

Some four hundred people can be counted attending the funeral of Jesús García.
Many more mourners undoubtedly are present outside the frame of the photograph
Courtesy of the Lewis W. Douglas Collection

James S. Douglas, general manager of the Moctezuma Copper Company, and the telegram he sent to his colleagues upon learning of the accident

Lewis W. Douglas at the Jesús García monument in Hermosillo.

Both photos courtesy of Lewis W. Douglas Collection

Francisco (Pancho) Villa and his army of Villistas campaigned along the
United States borders during Mexico's post-Revolution years
Courtesy of the Historical Collection of Herb and Dorothy McLaughlin

Above, refugees fled the mining
towns of Sonora during the
Great Depression of the 1930s
*Courtesy of the Historical
Collection of Herb and
Dorothy McLaughlin*

Right, the last American
steam train to leave
Nacozari in 1948
*Courtesy of the
Brophy Collection*

In Search of Jesús García

In Search of Jesús García

Another view of the American section of Nacozari that was taken after the erection of the Jesús García monument to the right *Author's Collection*

Norbert L. Sammelman, husband of a niece of Jesús García, some years ago traveled to Mexico to acquire a portfolio of monuments erected to the memory of the brave engineer. Above monument is in Veracruz, Mexico

Clockwise from above, Nacozari, Mexico City and Ciudad Obregón monuments

JESUS GARCIA.

EN ESTE LUGAR NACIO EL SOCIO
JESUS GARCIA HEROE DE NACOZARI
HUMILDE OBRERO
QUE INMORTALIZO SU NOMBRE
DANDO LA VIDA
POR SALVAR UN PUEBLO
SOCIEDAD ARTESANOS "HIDALGO"

Clockwise from left, Aguacalientes, Jesús García's birthplace at Hermosilla, San Luis Potosí, street in Mexico City, school in Hermosillo all show Mexico's respect for the "Hero of Nacozari"

William B. Barker, husband of another García relative, took his camera to the Sixtieth Anniversary, which was celebrated with special reverance. Above, dignitaries place a wreath at the place where the train exploded

As when the monument was dedicated in 1909, left, little girls of Nacozari in 1960
dressed as nurses who ministered to the injured following the great explosion
Left, Author's Collection; above, photo by Norbert L. Sammelman

Wreaths from Douglas are delivered by train for the 1960 celebration. Right, the pageant included a parade and serenade *Clockwise from above, photos by William B. Barker, Norbert L. Sammelman, William B. Barker*

In Search of Jesús García

In Search of Jesús García

Acknowledgments

The authors of this book are grateful for the inspiration, encouragement and information contributed by other celebrants of Mexico's brave railroader.

Glendon Swarthout of Scottsdale, Arizona, long ago suggested that Jesús García deserved an American-made book. Subsequent research drew upon the historical writings of Edward Gaylord Bourne, James Mitchell Clarke, Robert Glass Cleland, L. Terán Cuauhtémoc, Charles H. Dunning, George B. Eckhart, Odie B. Faulk, William Weber Johnson, Ira B. Joralemon, J. Patrick McHenry, Edward H. Peplow, Jr., Thomas C. Romney, C.L. Sonnichsen, Enguerrando Tapia and Paul Wilhelm. In the earlydays reporters of the *Douglas Daily Dispatch* kept faith with Nacozari's heroic happening. In later times writers associated with *The Arizona Republic* — Richard Barnes, Paul Dean, Frank Malone and Harold K. Milks — sustained interest in Nacozari. Elsewhere north of the border García gained attention of other feature writers, notably Judy Donovan of the *Arizona Daily Star,* John B. Hungerford of the *Los Angeles Times*, and Syd Love of the *San Diego Union*. And of course, uncounted numbers of signed and unsigned articles have appeared in the journals of Sonora and in such national publications as *Revista Ferronales (Railroad Review)*.

Also of assistance in this effort were Dr. Marvin Alisky, Center for Latin Studies, Arizona State University; William B. Barker of Carlsbad, California; Ervin Bond of Douglas, Arizona; A. Blake Brophy and Frank C. Brophy, Sr., of Phoenix, Arizona; Marguerite Cooley of the Arizona State Library and Archives; P. Allen Copeland of El Cajon, California; Peggy Damskey of Tucson, Arizona; Bill Epler of the *Brewery Gulch Gazette*, Bisbee, Arizona; Gloria Figueroa of Yuma, Arizona; Alfredo W. Kaldman of Nacozari; Professor Conrado Neblina García of San Luis, R.C., Sonora; Elizabeth McMillan, Litchfield Park, Arizona; David F. Myrick of San Francisco, California; Raul Ochoa of Nacozari; Susie Sato and Vicki Chavarria of the Arizona Historical Foundation, Hayden Library, Arizona State University, Tempe; Pat Scanlon of Phelps Dodge, Douglas; Winn

Smiley of the Arizona Historical Society; Rafael Urquides of Hermosillo, Sonora; Debbie Wilkens of Los Angeles, California; Ben F. Williams, Sr., of Douglas, Arizona; and John (Sandy) Wise of Hermosillo, Sonora. Particular thanks are extended to Dr. Robert P. Browder, chairman, department of history, University of Arizona, and to Donald M. Powell, chief special collections librarian, University of Arizona, Tucson. The patience of research assistant Cherie L. Dedera helped her across a hundred chuckholes up and down the road to Nacozari, and from the viewpoint of a Spanish language teacher, Annie Hays reviewed the manuscript.

For suffering through the doubled problems in printing a bilingual book, gratitude is expressed to Paul Weaver, Rick Stetter, James K. Howard, and Robert Jacobson of Northland Press, Flagstaff, Arizona. Photographic miracles were wrought by Walt Richee of Professional Photo Lab, Inc., of Phoenix; by Herb and Dorothy McLaughlin of Arizona Photographic Associates, Phoenix; and by Andy Lemke of Solano Beach Camera, Solano Beach, California. As credited, a number of the artistic, latter-day photographs of García monuments and celebrations are the work of Norbert L. Sammelman of Oceanside, California. His wife, Artemisa, a García niece, contributed facts and family photographs, as did nephews John R. Bartlett of Tucson, Ernest Bartlett of Yuma, and Herb Sanchez of Solano Beach.

All said, this book simply would not exist without the generous cooperation of members of the Douglas family. Through a period of research, the late Lewis W. Douglas urged the project along. His wife, Peggy Douglas of Tucson and New York City, kindly opened the Douglas family papers and albums for examination and reproduction. Lew Douglas' brother, James, of La Jolla, California (who recalls at age four hearing the explosion of García's train), was most helpful in resolving contradictions. The late George M. Douglas was an accomplished photographer as well as engineer at Nacozari during the early years of this century. Although now it is impossible to credit precisely, likely the better photographs of Nacozari environs are from the splendid camera of George Douglas.

While expressing thanks to all who gave assistance, the authors assume responsibility for whatever errors remain. Nearly seventy years after the explosion at Nacozari, the authors were not able to settle all conflicts of details.

Note to Acknowledgments 1989

This revised version of the Jesús García story might also had been in a bilingual format, but for the death of Bob Robles in 1988 in Phoenix. His was an artistic talent, the translation of English-Spanish faithful to the ear and intellect. That gift is not possessed by the surviving writer. As a compromise, passages of Bob Robles's Spanish are sprinkled here and there for a flavor of the Mexican language. As before, this book is dedicated to the people of Mexico and Americans of Mexican descent, but especially and affectionately, to the memory of Bob Robles.

Gratitude is felt toward those who encouraged the survivor onward. They are D I Bolding of North Hollywood, California; Bob Farrell of Phoenix, Arizona; Hugh Harelson of Phoenix; Vicky Hay of Phoenix; Wesley Holden of Phoenix; Armando Montaño, Nacozari; Gustavo Aldana-Montaño, Nacozari; Sam Negri of Phoenix; Delia Sánchez of Phoenix; Rosemary and Dick Totman of Scottsdale, Arizona; Downs Matthews of Houston, Texas; Sally Robles of Phoenix; Guillermo Hernández-Silva, presidente of Nacozari; Daisy and Ben Williams, Jr. of Douglas, Arizona and Marilyn and Jack Yelverton of Belvedere, California.

Special thanks are extended to Northland Press of Flagstaff, Arizona, publisher of *Goodbye, García, Adiós,* for relinquishing rights to make this book possible.

Deserving of special thanks are the Dons Club of Arizona and Tony Subia, owner of the Subiacolor photographic laboratory of Phoenix. It happened that much of Nacozari's history was lost when American companies withdrew from Mexico. From various sources Subiacolor produced a quality portfolio of images dating to the life and times of Jesús García. The portfolio was hand delivered by the Dons Club and presented to Nacozari's newly founded town museum on November 7, 1989.

Bibliography

Alisky, Marvin. "Surging Sonora," *Arizona Highways* magazine, November, 1964.

Almada, Francisco R. *Diccionario de Historia, Geográfia y Biográfia* Sonorenses, Chihuahua, Chihuahua: Fernandez, 1977.

Barnes, Richard. "Memory of Heroic Engineer is Honored by People He Died to Save from Explosion," the *Brewery Gulch Gazette*, May 4, 1961.

Chisholm, Joe. "Dr. James Douglas," the *Arizona Historical Review*, Volume 4, 1931-32.

Cleland, Robert Glass. *A History of Phelps Dodge*, New York: A. A. Knopf, 1952.

Dean, Paul, "Passage of Time Dulls Mexican Rail Legend," *The Arizona Republic*, January 20, 1976.

Dedera, Don. "Mexican Railroader Rode His Dynamite Train to Glory," the San Diego *Evening Tribune*, November 6, 1982.

—————— . "In Search of Jesús García," *Exxon USA* magazine, first quarter, 1977.

—————— . "By Golly, You Can Get There from Here," *Outdoor Arizona* magazine, November, 1975.

—————— . "A Tiny Town Remembers His Courage," the *San Diego Union*, November 8, 1964.

—————— , and Bob Robles. *Goodbye, García, Adiós,* Flagstaff: Northland Press, 1976.

Diaz del Castillo, Bernal. *The Discovery and Conquest of Mexico*, New York: Farrar, Straus and Cudahy, 1956.

Donovan, Judy. "Jesus García: Mexican Folk Hero," the *Arizona Daily Star* November 2, 1975.

Douglas, Lewis W. (Brief Jesús García item), *Reader's Digest*, November, 1948.

Dunning, Charles H. with Edward H. Peplow, Jr. *Rock to Riches,* Phoenix: Southwest Publishing Company, Inc., 1959.

Eckhart, George B. "A Guide to the History of the Missions of Sonora," *Arizona and the West*, Volume VI, Number Two, 1960.

Epler, Bill. "Mexico Sells Nacozari Copper Complex, Cananea Is Next," *Pay Dirt* magazine, November, 1988.

Griffith, Jim. Book review, the *Journal of Arizona History,* Winter, 1976.

Hanson, Joseph Mills. "Jesús García," *Frontier Ballads*, Chicago: A.C. McClurg and Company, 1910.

Hungerford, John B. "Mexico's Own Casey Jones," the *Los Angeles Times*, January 20, 1958.

Johnson, William Weber. *Heroic Mexico*, Garden City: Doubleday & Company, Inc., 1968.

Joralemon, Ira B. *Copper; The Encompassing Story of Mankind's First Metal*, Berkeley: Howell-North Books, 1973.

Knight, Susan M. "Teacher Uses a Hero to Better Attitudes," the *Arizona Daily Star*, November 22, 1982.

Lancaster, Cindy. "Yuman's Book Records Bravery of National Hero of Mexico," the *Yuma Daily Sun*, September 2, 1976.

Love, Syd. "The Hero of Nacozari Still Lives in the Hearts of Mexico," the *San Diego Union*, December 14, 1975.

Malone, Frank. "Jesús García Day," *Arizona Magazine, The Arizona Republic*, December 12, 1971.

Milks, Harold K. "La Caridad to Aid Economy," *The Arizona Republic*, November 29, 1970.

Negri, Sam. "Hero of Nacozari," *The Arizona Republic*, November 19, 1982.

Powell, Donald M. "Bookshelf," *Arizona Highways* magazine, February, 1977.

Rees, Dave. "Jesús García Day Honors a Brave Man," *Pay Dirt* magazine, November 21, 1971.

Riding, Alan. *Distant Neighbors, a Portrait of the Mexicans,* New York: Alfred A. Knopf, 1984.

Romney, Thomas C. "The Savior of Nacozari," typescript, Douglas Collection, Tucson, October 13, 1950.

Sonnichsen, C.L. *Colonel Greene and the Copper Skyrocket,* Tucson: the University of Arizona Press, 1974.

Teran, L. Cuauhtemoc. *Jesus Garcia, el Heroe de Nacozari, Mexico* Mexico City: Publicidad Creativa, S.A., 1962

Weber, David J. *Myth and History of the Hispanic Southwest*, Albuquerque: the University of New Mexico Press, 1987.

Williams, J.S., Jr. Untitled, brief history of Nacozari operations, typescript, Phelps Dodge archives, Phoenix, Arizona, 1922.

Young, Herbert V. "The Douglas Family," *Ghosts of Cleopatra Hill*, Jerome, Arizona: The Jerome Historical Society, 1960.

Young, William S., editor. "Porter's Production," *Steam Locomotive* magazine, April, 1960.

Zarbin, Earl. "Anza: Frontier Explorer," *The Arizona Republic,* September 28, 1975.

Unsigned. "Heroism of Engineer Saves Nacozari," the *Douglas [Arizona] International-American,* November 8, 1907.

Unsigned. "Engineer's Bravery Saves Many Lives," the *Arizona Daily Star,* Tucson, November 9, 1907.

Unsigned. "The Sacrifice of Jesús García, Railroad Hero of Nacozari," *Illinois Central* magazine, November, 1966.

Unsigned. "A Man Who Died to Save a Town," *New York Times,* circa 1909.

Unsigned. "The 'Casey Jones of Mexico,'" *Railway Journal,* November, 1976.

Unsigned. *Gesto Heróico de Jesús García Corona, Revista Nacozari* magazine, October 30, 1975.

Unsigned. *Datos Biográficos de Jesús García Corona. Revista Nacozari* magazine, July 14, 1975.

Unsigned. "Jesús García, the Hero of Nacozari," *Tracks, the Chesapeake and Ohio Railway Magazine,* Volume 34, Number Four, April, 1950

Index

Books by Don Dedera

A Mile in His Moccasins, 1960

Anybody Here from Arizona:
   A Look at the Vietnam War, 1966

Explorer's Guide to the West (Ten Chapters), 1973

Arizona the Beautiful, 1973

Hang Gliding: The Flyingest Flying, 1975

Navajo Rugs: How to Find, Evaluate, Buy
   and Care for Them, 1975

Goodbye, García, Adiós, 1976

Discover Arizona Uplands, 1979

Visions West: The Story of the Cowboy Artists
   of America Museum, 1983

Arizona's Scenic Seasons (Text Editor), 1983

In Coronado's Footsteps (Editor), 1983

Artistry in Clay, 1985

Eileen Monaghan Whitaker Paints San Diego, 1986

The Cactus Sandwich,
   and other Tall Tales of the Southwest, 1986

A Little War of Our Own:
   The Pleasant Valley Feud Revisited, 1988

The Storyteller: Art of Howard Terpning, 1989

In Search of Jesús García, 1989